MIND HOW YOU GO

There has never been a book written about driver attitudes like this one. It is a philosophy about how to think when driving a motor vehicle.

MIND HOW YOU GO contains information never published before, and includes techniques about how to think in all driving situations.

It shows you how to avoid situations where you are forced to react and illustrates how to think ahead, then act for a reason.

Even if you don't read the whole of this book, what you do read will change your outlook and attitudes towards your driving life and you will be safer for it. Not only that, you will find this book both entertaining and informative.

We invite you to make your own mind up and take responsibility for yourself.

That is what this book can do for you.

Think before you act

and

MIND HOW YOU GO

Acknowledgements

The authors would like to thank the following for their contributions towards making this book possible. Darren Brown, David Bushell, Graham Butterfield, Marie Clapham, Paul Dixon, David Etchells, Tony Garner, Christopher and Sheelagh Grundy, Stephen Hall, George Hunt, Dave Jones, Susan Law, Brian McClair, Barry Putson, Michelle Slater, Paul Smith, Chris Sulley, Stephen Waddington, Dr Fran Walsh, Craig Waters, and finally Barbara and Margaret for their patience and endless cups of tea.

First published in Great Britain by
Ashdon Woodlight Publishing

MIND HOW YOU GO

Published by Ashdon Woodlight Publishing
Printed and Bound by The Amadeus Press, Cleckheaton

ISBN 978-0-9554597-0-2

www.mindhowyougo.co.uk

Front Cover Photograph *taken from the highest bridge on Great Britain's highest motorway, the M62, where it crosses the Pennines approximately half way between Manchester and Leeds.*

All Photographs © Adrian Shurmer 2006

Index

SECTION 1 — **7**

An introduction into how and why this 'driver thinking' book originated

SECTION 2 — **11**

A synopsis of poor driver attitudes and how previous
and established driver knowledge has become submerged
by bureaucratic, ill-conceived measures and inconsistency

SECTION 3 — **25**

Developing an attitude
An innovative guide about how to think in a driving sense
whilst keeping within the law, and how to become aware of both good and bad
situations in order to take responsibility for yourself

SECTION 4 — **65**

Motorway driving
Much of this information has never been published before

SECTION 5 — **109**

Be ahead of the game
Security (VIP Protection) attitudes and techniques
and similarities between aware driving and all sporting activity

SECTION 6 — **119**

Driver Awareness summary

SECTION 7 — **123**

'What do you think?'
An exposure of inconsistent road traffic measures where
the question is asked, 'What do you think, now that you
have received an insight into aware driver thinking?'

SECTION 8 — **145**

Driver Awareness quiz and answers

SECTION 9 — **161**

Authorities in need of education
Conclusion

About the Authors

Adrian Shurmer

I was a British police driving instructor in the 1980s and I also taught VIP protection drivers how to think and handle pressure situations so as to remain as safe as possible.

As far as I am aware, I became the only police driving instructor who had never been attached to a police traffic department. I looked at life, and my job, in a different way to my colleagues. I was more interested in driver attitudes rather than physical driving skills.

In those days, I realised there was a huge gap between what my students were taught about driving and what the general public knew. Until 1990, British Police 'Class One' drivers were the most highly trained drivers in the world. Our police driving training establishments set the highest standards and 'British Police Trained' was a description that immediately commanded respect.

Sadly, this no longer applies. Over recent years, due mainly to political influence, ill-thought out reorganisations and cutbacks within the police driving establishments, standards of police driving have fallen into severe decline.

Contrary to popular belief there is a *new way*, a very effective and successful way to approach road safety matters.

In order to try to improve matters, especially with regard to VIP protection driving attitudes and techniques, I realised that 'driver thinking' was more important than teaching physical driving skills and I established a business to promote these attitudes. This is what I do now. Since 1992, Driver Awareness Courses, on which this book is based, have helped companies save many hundreds of thousands of pounds in insurance costs by cutting the accident rate among their fleet of drivers.

Driver Awareness Limited is not a driving school, so if you are looking for a book about current (and inadequate) advanced driving techniques, you have picked up the wrong book.

This book suggests that there is a new way to approach the delicate and personal subject of driver education. We are all experts and can benefit by increasing our expertise. When we know how to think, driving can become (serious) fun, by turning negatives into positives and adopting the attitude that when other road users are behaving themselves, it's only a bonus.

The advice within this book is more of a driving philosophy. This is VIP protection for everyday drivers; after all there is no greater VIP than yourself.

Steve O'Donnell

'Stay calm, courteous and considerate.' Those were my Dad's final words of advice as I left to take my driving test, aged 17 years and three weeks.

He had taught me how to drive when I was about eight years old; me sitting on his knees in a Land-Rover, steering and 'doing the gears', whilst he pressed the pedals, driving up and down farm tracks and across the fields at the bottom of our garden at home, avoiding sheep, trees and ditches. When I grew taller, I was allowed to press the pedals as well, and I quickly became very comfortable behind a wheel.

My first job after leaving school, aged 16, was with a road haulage company, whose fleet included oil tankers, articulated lorries, rigid flat-bed wagons and the like. As the premises were on private land, I drove anything and everything that needed to be moved around the loading bays and parking areas, so that by the time it came to take my driving test I had driven a greater variety of vehicles than most people would drive in a lifetime.

This experience proved to be invaluable, as it quickly taught me how to assess the different characteristics of each vehicle.

'Be aware of what's going on around you' 'always expect the unexpected' and 'drive within the vehicle's capabilities' are some of the other things my Dad drummed into me, and his advice has stayed with me ever since. It all seems like common sense, yet every day our roads are full of drivers who do not adhere to these principles, and that is why this book has been written.

MIND HOW YOU GO is a valuable book because it explains an attitude and offers driving tips that can help save lives, avoid serious injuries and save millions of pounds.

We want to do something about making your motoring life a safer one. You have to be prepared to take the initiative. You are reading this, which shows you are off to a great start.

If you are sitting comfortably, we will get our journey of discovery underway.

> ## *If you sort out 'the mind', the physical skills will look after themselves*

What people say

Every now and again a book comes along that is unique and, at the same time, informative, practical, witty, thought provoking and potentially life saving. This book fits this description. Adrian Shurmer, a colourful, larger than life character, with vast knowledge and experience of driving awareness has made it a "must have" book for all drivers, but particularly any young learner or inexperienced newcomer to the wheel. The amount of knowledge in this book and the insight to the world of motoring is staggering. If you thought you knew about driving - think again! This book takes the reader into a completely different league of driving awareness compared to your average publication.

As a person who has worked within the professional football industry for several years, I know how difficult it is to make an impression on young footballers who are starting out on a career that could bring them fame and considerable fortune. Adrian Shurmer was able not only to attract and hold their attention when he worked with them here at Bolton Wanderers F.C., but he had the lads and our senior staff, including our drivers, hanging on his every word and importantly was able to change their mindset with respect to their approach to driving.

His enthusiasm and incisive knowledge of the subject matter is second to none; he is the consummate professional. His delivery, on the course he laid on for our young players, was done in a very honest and humorous way, which is replicated in this book, and this is why I am prepared and delighted to recommend and comment on it.

Dr Fran Walsh,
Head of Education and Welfare, Bolton Wanderers Football Club.

At Manchester United, we have also been involved in the 'Shurmer Experience' and I totally concur with everything that Fran has said above. Adrian stimulates the boys to think that, as in football, the physical and technical are important, but without good habits and awareness, the opportunities for success are less.

David Bushell,
Head of Education and Welfare, Manchester United Football Club.

Two days of advice about Driver Awareness is like a lifetime of re-eduction, not on how to drive, more on how to think, look and behave, and help you to gain precious seconds in today's high speed battle ground we used to call the highway.
All our sales team have discovered the art of Driver Awareness and in the years since the Course, our accident rate has dropped to almost nil.

Graham Butterfield,
Sales Director, Silentnight Beds

Introduction

Foreword

The reason for writing this book is to introduce a unique and radical method of driver education. It is not just about physical driving skills; it is more to do with how to think.

We live by the motto; 'Sort out the mind and the physical will look after itself.'

The problems which many drivers encounter, especially young drivers, are attributable to their cavalier attitude to life and their misguided belief that they are immortal. For those reasons, we believe that the most effective way to improve road safety is through education; not just by improving their physical driving skills, but through well presented information which will enable every driver to make better and more reasoned decisions.

We take the view that the present government policy and system towards improving road safety is a failure. How else can these policies be described when an average of nine deaths and 120 serious injuries occur on our roads each day? There must be a solution to this very serious problem. From the examples shown and discussed in this book, the methods currently employed by the authorities to improve road safety are pitiful.

The authorities in this country follow an inane system where, in an effort to improve things, they know no better than to build hazards in front of drivers who are already colliding with hazards. Then they unnecessarily narrow the road carriageway, thus increasing the risk of collision for everyone.

It is said that 'Speed Kills', and there is no denying the fact that the faster a vehicle collides with an object, the greater the risk of serious injury to the driver and passengers. But this slogan is incomplete. What is true is that 'Speed kills when it is used by the wrong people in the wrong place.'

Following on from this point, 'speed cameras' are not the answer when it comes to improving safety on the road. They are a distraction, and contribute to increasing the risk of danger. We take the view that they are part of a government policy of exploitation. How else can they be described, when the motoring public have had to suffer over £700 million in fines since they were introduced in 1993, yet the accident (crash) statistics on our roads show little improvement. Speed cameras have not solved the problem of road safety because speed in itself is not the problem.

The lack of proper driver education is the real problem.

If we are going to educate drivers, especially young and inexperienced drivers, we need to treat them with respect, and the information provided must be consistent, well presented, and based on simplicity and common sense.

We must spend more time and energy as parents and as a society, to teach our young people to take driving seriously and to make sure they are properly licensed before allowing them behind the wheel. We must teach our children to respect the dangers of excessive speed and to accept responsibility for their own safety and the safety of their friends, family and other road users.

Driver education should start at school, around the age of 15 years, and for those who did not have this opportunity, there should be classes at adult education centres.

Driver awareness can be fun and entertaining. It is not a dull subject and if it comes across as such, then the ability and knowledge of the teacher should be questioned. Dull teachers, ill-informed authorities and inappropriate information are all part of the current system. It's time for a change. After all, there is no more worthy a cause than to protect life and reduce serious injuries.

To an aware driver, there is nothing simpler than keeping a vehicle in as much s p a c e as possible, adopting the attitude of complete non-trust towards other road users, and maintaining the belief that 'when other road users are behaving themselves, it's only a bonus.'

MIND HOW YOU GO can alter your whole view on life. It is about the choices you can make for yourself when you are driving. Instead of relying on other people, or being forced by them to do something that you don't want to do, you are in a position to make your own decisions.

MIND HOW YOU GO does not issue rules for you to follow; it gives advice. The reasons behind the advice are explained. In order for you to do what is safe, you need to know both why you are doing it, and the consequences of not doing it.

It is hard to overstate how pleasant it is to be the passenger in a car when the driver is calm and in full control. The act of driving appears effortless and easy, and this is only achieved by concentration and planning. The aware driver constantly updates and modifies his driving plan to meet the changing road and traffic conditions.

Welcome to
MIND HOW YOU GO

> **MIND** HOW YOU GO *is not so much how to drive, more a way in which to think when you are driving. When people have knowledge, they are in a position to make better and more reasoned decisions*

A synopsis of Poor Driver Attitudes

' The majority of drivers are simply not aware of the potential dangers on everyday roads.
Why should they be? No one has ever pointed them out. '

A synopsis of Poor Driver Attitudes

How previous and established driver knowledge has become submerged by bureaucratic, ill-conceived measures and inconsistency.

If you were to ask a cross section of drivers 'What is the most important factor in making you safer and more aware of the dangers on the road?' you would get a variety of responses.

Most would shrug and look blank. If an answer came at all it would invariably be 'Observation.' This is a good answer, but not the correct one.

If the dead could speak or a survey was carried out amongst those seriously injured as a result of crashes, most would say that they saw the other vehicle or hazard prior to the actual collision.

What could be more important than observation?

The answer is simple. Educate drivers, which will help to increase their awareness.

A learner driver is taught co-ordination of mind and body and thereby develops particular skills. The eyes see, the brain transmits and the body reacts. Good judgment is enhanced with experience and the correct attitude.

Experience comes with time, but the correct attitude can be introduced immediately.

Poor driver attitudes contribute to more accidents than a lack of driving skills. In everyday driving, attitude and judgment are inseparable. Judgment is the individual's ability to recognise actual and potential dangers in advance and keep their vehicle in a safe position at all times, so that a loss of control or a crash is avoidable.

Attitude cannot be defined easily. Here are some examples of bad attitude, which are common to many drivers.

Eight blunders of the world

Look at these driver characteristics and see if you recognise them. The common characteristic is poor driver thinking.

(1) **Lack of Consideration:** The picture says it all.

(2) **Over-confidence:** People who take too much for granted. These drivers are confident that they can control their vehicle under any circumstances. They fail to allow for the actions of others, from motorists to pedestrians or animals.

(3) **Pride:** This characteristic overlaps with over-confidence. Statements such as 'I've never been involved in an accident.' are frequently heard from this group. Cemeteries are full of people who have died as a result of their first accident.

(4) **Experience:** They have been driving for years and their mantra is 'I don't think there is anything you can show me about driving.' This experience is wonderful. It divinely sees them through all types of road and traffic situations, or so they think. The truth is, experience can develop as many bad habits as good ones.

(5) **Impatience:** People who take chances. Look in the dictionary under 'chance' and you'll find words like accidental, risky, fate and gamble. To gamble is to wager, to venture into the unknown, to plunge or to speculate. Impatient people spend a great deal of time manufacturing tight situations for themselves, taking short-cuts, abusing traffic queues, accelerating harshly and frequently braking too hard and too late.

(6) **Abuse of the Vehicle:** This group overworks the brakes, or changes down into a lower gear at too high a speed and constantly over-rev the engine. They bump over kerb edges, scrub the tyre walls and fail to slow down when negotiating uneven road surfaces. Then, when they suffer a breakdown, they complain that the vehicle has failed them.

> *It's not the vehicle that lets you down;*
> *it's YOU who lets the vehicle down*

(7) **Slow Drivers:** We are referring here to car drivers and not LGV drivers who sometimes have to be the slower driver. Slow car drivers can be a danger to themselves and others. They will drive at a speed well below the posted speed limit and are oblivious to the queue growing behind them. Slow drivers create frustration. That can lead to others driving too close and taking unacceptable risks in order to pass them. If challenged about their driving, the slow drivers claim they are simply being careful. However, it is more likely that they are unable to deal with modern-day levels of traffic. Even more worrying, their eyesight may not meet the Department of Transport criteria. If you should find yourself behind one of these slow drivers accept the situation, be patient and reduce your frustration. Concentrate at all times and remain safe.

(8) **Dangles and Distractions:** Dangles are those furry rabbits, dice, beads, perfumed Christmas trees and so on that hang from a driver's interior rear-view mirror. How can it be possible for any driver to concentrate fully and to be conscientious and responsible when something is swinging about right in front of their eyes? They will often have large obstructions in the rear window as well, such as 'L' plates or 'Baby on Board' stickers, which restrict the available view through the window. Then there are the drivers you see preening themselves in the mirror. Still others have a habit of driving and at the same time looking sideways at their passengers whilst carrying on a conversation. The same applies when a driver is illegally using a hand-held mobile telephone.

MIND HOW YOU GO *takes the view that vehicle windows are for looking through. Why obstruct them unnecessarily? Lives can be put at risk by reducing the areas of vision*

For instance, the next time you see another vehicle sticking religiously to the middle lane of a motorway, or a vehicle stopping at a roundabout when the road ahead is clear, or the driver behaving in any other irresponsible manner, you will probably see one of the driver characteristics mentioned and gain a good insight into the attitude of that driver.

There are many examples of poor driver attitude and you can draw up your own list of pet hates. The ones covered here are typically found on the roads and motorways of Britain today.

We can all think of someone who falls into one or more of these categories without much effort. You may even recognise yourself. If so, perhaps you should ask yourself what is gained from your actions and whether they are constructive. Fortunately, negative driving attitudes are neither inbred nor inherited, they are created. They evolve and become reinforced through repetition. They can be eliminated.

Educating the Driver

If you sort out 'the mind', the physical skills will generally look after themselves.

Anyone can be involved in a crash. We are human and therefore make mistakes. Drivers lose concentration but there is more to it than that. The majority of drivers are simply not aware of the potential dangers on everyday roads. Why should they be? No one has ever pointed them out.

When we learn to drive we are taught to control a vehicle, but we need more guidance. Drivers should be advised on certain basic common sense applications to help with their driving. This will be discussed in greater detail later in this book.

On top of the ability to control a vehicle, you need to develop greater awareness of the actual and potential dangers you face every day. This knowledge will improve your driving, your safety, the safety of your passengers and the other road users around you.

The authors of this book have a unique approach towards imparting information, especially in relation to driver awareness. We appreciate that everyone reading this book is to some degree, an expert. All we are trying to do is increase your expertise.

MIND HOW YOU GO *gives advice to make you think about things more*

Answer these questions of yourself;

- Have you ever received driver education about how to overtake correctly?
- Have you ever received any advice about driving in all weather conditions?
- Have you ever received any advice about how to think when driving along country lanes?
- Have you ever received any advice about night time driving?
- Have you ever received any advice about driver attitude and awareness techniques?
- Have you ever received any advice about motorway driving attitudes and techniques, from an experienced police motorway patrol officer?

When you are driving on the roads, it is important to be aware of the hazards that surround you.

That is why it is essential to develop good habits to safeguard **yourself.**

If you have the desire to increase your awareness when you are driving, you will need to gain knowledge. Once you have started to gain knowledge, your skill will increase, and having increased your skill, you will find you will want to gain further knowledge. It's a full circle, and your habits will become self-generating.

By adopting the attitudes and advice given in this book you will improve your own safety and that of others on the road and by doing so, you will help to relieve congestion and pollution.

Just think, if the methods shown in this book became an integral part of the driver education programme given to those whose responsibility it is to teach others to drive, congestion and pollution would decrease immediately.

Every accident involves emotional stresses, strains and in some cases, severe trauma, whether through the tragic loss of life or merely the anger and frustration caused by the delay that these incidents create.

In addition to having to bear the consequential effects of higher insurance premiums as a result of these accidents, there are other knock-on effects that bald statistics do not reveal.

MIND HOW YOU GO is all about driver thinking and offers you advice on how to take a closer look at the causes of many accidents. What this book will reveal is that there are few accidents, only crashes.

To make this clear, let us examine the definition of the word 'accident.'

'An event proceeding from an unknown cause.'

'The unforeseen effect of a known cause.'

'Something unexpected.'

The word 'accident' is being used at this stage because when you know how to think as an aware driver, these accidents will become crashes.

What is an accident?

If you are walking along a road and a branch of a tree breaks off and falls on you; that is an accident.

When you analyse accidents that occur on our roads however, you will see that at least one driver will have made an assumption regarding the actions of another driver.

To make this point clear:

Most drivers assume that a vehicle waiting in a side road will not move out in front of them.

Most drivers assume that a child on the footpath will not run into the road.

Most drivers assume that doors of parked vehicles will not open in front of them when they drive along narrow streets or roadways.

Most drivers assume that on open roads, oncoming vehicles will not pull out on an overtaking manoeuvre from the opposite direction and occupy their part of the carriageway.

Most drivers assume and trust other road users, whereas, such trust is anathema to an aware driver.

The golden rule is; 'Never Assume'

With this in mind, here are some of the reasons given by drivers involved in 'accidents'

- The weather was to blame; whether it was fog, snow, black ice, heavy rain, bright sunshine, extremely windy conditions or any combination of the above.

- A dog or cat suddenly ran onto the road.

- A wasp or a bee flew into the vehicle through an open window.

- My foot had slipped off the brake pedal, because I had stepped in a patch of oil.

Human nature is such that people always blame each other, no matter what the circumstances or situation. When a police officer is called to attend an incident on the road, one common factor will invariably run throughout his report. It will always be claimed that 'the other driver' was to blame.

When a motorist has emerged from a side road into the path of a vehicle on the main road, that driver will always accuse the driver of the vehicle on the main road of travelling too fast.

When two vehicles collide at a set of traffic lights, each driver will blame the other for going through the lights on red.

There are thousands of incidents like these and each one has a common denominator; it was always the other driver's fault.

The one thing you should learn from all this is not to be there in the first place and to keep yourself out of trouble. It doesn't matter who was to blame.

> ## It is better not to be involved at all than to say, 'It wasn't my fault'

Motorists are constantly warned about stretches of 'dangerous roads' and 'dangerous bends' where accidents have happened in the past

Which of these photographs of the same stretch of road represents a dangerous road?

The answer is neither of them; it's drivers on the road who are dangerous

And then we have modern design together with technological advances, which have improved our vehicles by introducing such things as safety cages, impact crumple zones, side impact bars, airbags, traction control and ABS braking systems. In the main we have good roads with signs and road markings. Various speed limits have been introduced, designed to reduce danger and the government has also introduced legislation making the wearing of seat belts mandatory. In addition to this, there are numerous traffic laws and a police force to uphold those laws, together with radar traps, mobile and static speed cameras which are used to catch motorists who exceed the posted speed limit. These measures have addressed our roads, our vehicles and the way the law is enforced.

What else can be done? Rather than continue in this vein we must first look at the one thing we have ignored...

THE DRIVER

The driver is the one constant in every crash, though when the authorities, highway agencies, and planners look at new measures to introduce in an effort to reduce the number of crashes, how often do they focus on the driver's thought processes and attitudes? Rarely.

The truth of the matter is that to 'instruct' a driver is a very personal matter, and has to be handled with care.

As we said earlier, an accident is caused by something unknown, unforeseen or unexpected. The word 'unplanned' in this context is very interesting. Vehicles cannot plan, roads cannot plan and the weather, as we know to our cost, cannot be planned. The only element involved in planning is the driver, and drivers do not plan to crash their vehicles.

It is clear that crashes occur when drivers do not have a plan of action when on the road. Therefore the logical progression, rather than instruct, is to advise the driver of the benefits of planning their journeys. This will create good habits, and educate them about how to think when driving.

As we have seen, crashes are blamed on a variety of things and normally overlook the actions of the individual behind the steering wheel. While various measures and campaigns are introduced at an enormous cost each year, little attention is given to improving the driver's education.

A more detailed examination of some of the measures that have been taken to try to cut down accidents only underlines that driver education, as an essential ingredient, is being ignored.

Let us look at some of these measures and see how effective they have been.

Traffic-calming measures

This is a typical scene where a council has constructed red strips across the road, pavement build-outs with black metal posts, incomplete cycle lanes, white paint and red paint road marking and bus stops opposite one another. In other words, anything and everything except addressing the driver education problem.

This picture exposes the naivety of most traffic calming measures and road markings implemented by councils following government guidelines. As you will read later in this book, aware drivers are advised that the most beneficial place to be on the approach to a right hand bend, is into the left-hand side of the road. They will also be aware that most other drivers only drive on what they can see. So here we have white paint, which encourages drivers to drive in the middle of the road on the approach to a right hand bend. The white paint on the opposite side, on the apex of the bend, encourages drivers into near head-on collisions, especially in poor visibility.

The slogan 'Speed Kills' was a memorable one. The effect it had was to inspire the ill thought-out traffic calming measures introduced by local authorities over the years.

It was naive to think that the only solution to the high accident numbers was to slow traffic down by placing additional hazards in the way of drivers, particularly when those very drivers are already colliding with existing ones. Adding another hazard is simply adding another danger.

Traffic calming measures come in all shapes and sizes. There are chicanes, the narrowing of lanes, additional paving build-outs into the road and cycle lanes that disappear as suddenly as they start. Whichever method is chosen, the idea to try and reduce vehicle speed by adding more hazards to an already potentially dangerous situation brings with it new problems.

The majority of these projects produced two negative effects. Firstly, they brought road users closer together and secondly, they have brought traffic and pedestrians closer together.

Some of the initiatives are ludicrous and inconsistent. When the police train their own drivers, the instruction given to the driver is always to give cyclists a side-on wobble distance of six feet (two metres) whilst overtaking them. Why then do the authorities allow the councils to paint cycle lanes on many of our roads that are less than four feet wide?

Here is another example of a council folly. The law states that all vehicles must display parking lights when stationary and unattended on a road, or in a lay-by on a road, with a speed limit greater than 30 mph. Why then has this council, apparently with police approval, constructed parking bays inside a 40 mph area, thereby encouraging drivers to park their vehicles, without lights, all night long and break the law?

Speed cameras

The speed camera policy in this country does little to improve road safety.

The popular phrase used is **'Speed Kills'** and it is clear that in the event of a collision, the faster the speed, the more serious the consequences. However, if you try and define the word 'speed', you will have great difficulty.

The one word missing from this phrase is 'inappropriate.' What should be made clear is that **'inappropriate speed kills.'**

Speed kills when the wrong people use it in the wrong place. In other words, excessive and inappropriate speed is a driver education problem.

For example: If you drive past a school at 8.30am, when there are children in the immediate vicinity, driving at 20 mph can be regarded as dangerous and reckless. However, drive past the same spot at 8.30pm when there are no children around, and 30 mph and above can be perfectly safe, although we no not advocate abusing a posted speed limit.

Therefore road safety is a matter of driver education, but how is education to become the main issue when, as this book demonstrates, our government doesn't know what to do?

Speeding and crashes occur in different places at different times. As part of normal human behaviour, drivers tend to increase their speed when the road is clear.

Some 12 million motorists have been convicted of speeding by speed cameras since the first tickets were issued around 1993. Over £700 million has been raised in speeding fines but our roads are no safer and road deaths have not fallen significantly for over a decade. At the time of writing there is an average of nine people killed on our roads each day and a further 120 seriously injured. This carnage should not continue any further.

The majority of motorists who receive a speeding ticket, especially when they know they were driving at a safe and appropriate speed at the time of the alleged offence, feel bitter and aggrieved. What can this do for road safety attitudes when motorists resent these exploitative measures and feel abused? And what does it do for road safety attitudes when drivers now spend most of their driving time looking out for cameras and staring at their speedometers, instead of looking at the road ahead and using their mirrors?

The problem is that some speed cameras have been positioned to impose speed limits which are often inappropriate for the area. Speed cameras can occasionally be useful servants towards improving road safety, but they are increasingly becoming a cruel and incompetent master.

Whilst most drivers exceed the speed limits on occasion, only a tiny minority exceed a safe speed with significant frequency.

Excessive and automated enforcement, with no regard to the conditions which prevail, has turned our speed limit laws into a national joke. It has become a ridiculous and highly counterproductive game of evasion and capture. The competent and careful actions of the majority of responsible drivers should not be considered illegal.

We are learning a hard and difficult lesson. There is nothing wrong with the speed limit laws, but since they are highly arbitrary in nature they need to be enforced with intelligence and discretion. This is what our skilled police traffic officers used to provide before speed cameras came along. It is the change in enforcement practice that has caused all the trouble.

After all, you don't need a speedometer to drive safely and you can't measure safe driving in miles per hour.

Developing an Attitude

Developing an attitude

Having an attitude is not a problem. When it comes to driving, having an aware attitude might just save your life. An aware attitude is the fundamental attribute of this entire driving philosophy.

It can help you to change the way you think when you get into a car and help to change the habits of a lifetime driving, in a positive way.

What does developing an aware attitude, or becoming a driver with attitude, actually mean? It means changing your habits so that you can keep your vehicle in a safe position on the road at all times, whether you are travelling at speed on a busy motorway or stopped in traffic. To help to change your habits, there is one crucial belief you have to keep in mind at all times.

> ## You need to think that all other road users are incompetent and sometimes irresponsible

Start thinking like that and you will be a driver with an aware attitude because it will have a direct effect on how you physically drive.

Do not get the wrong idea. This is not a doctrine for slow, timid or even negative driving. Neither is it an aggressive approach, although drivers with an aware attitude always command their position on the road.

And it is not about speed. Speed is not the object. Anyone can drive fast. A driver with an aware attitude is a driver who is thinking, he is the one who can make real progress. It is not simply a case of keeping the accelerator pedal pressed flat to the floor and hoping for the best.

Having an aware attitude in this respect is progressive and positive. It puts you in constant control.

Starting blocks

Step one towards achieving the correct attitude when driving is simple. You have to have an unshakeable belief that every other road user is a real danger. They fall into one or more of the following categories: unskilled, arrogant, indifferent, irresponsible, bad mannered and criminal.

Most drivers are generally unskilled. They haven't had the benefit of further driver education or training. This does not mean we are advocating being unkind to fellow humans who find themselves behind a wheel. If road users thought of each other as belonging to one or all of the above categories, there would be far fewer crashes.

The argument is simple. How much training does the average driver receive? Can you honestly say that when you passed your test you had been taught how to overtake both safely and correctly? Did you drive in all weather conditions before you passed your test? Did you ever receive advice about the attitudes needed for driving along country lanes? Did you ever have the benefit of any night time driving tuition? Have you ever had any driver attitude or awareness education or know anyone who has received specific education about how to drive on a motorway by someone with police training and knowledge?

You may be lucky. You may have answered yes to one or more of those questions. That puts you in a select band of people. The majority of the driving population of this country would have said no to all of them. These people may have passed a driving test, but they are unskilled in various aspects of driving and knowing this will change the way you begin to look at your fellow motorists.

You do not need to be in a car to see how bad mannered, arrogant and criminal society in general has become. Just pick up a newspaper and you have all the evidence you need.

This combination of limited driving education and poor standards of behaviour within our society is a potentially lethal cocktail that takes to our roads every day.

How do we spot the worst offenders? The simple answer is not to bother looking, just consider that they are all as bad as one another.

This ethos is based on police VIP protection driving attitudes and techniques. The police realise that burglars don't wander the streets in masks and stripy shirts carrying bags marked 'Swag', and that bad drivers do not have 'Dangerous' or 'Poor Driver' stickers on their bumpers.

> ## When other road users are behaving themselves, it's only a bonus.

The VIP

When you are entrusted with the safety of a VIP you quickly develop a mind set. You trust no one. You don't know where the threat will come from. That way no one can surprise you. That is the approach you need to take every day. The next time you drive, ask yourself who is the VIP in your life who needs protecting? If this technique is good enough for royalty then surely it is good enough for you. Remember, the VIP is you and each of your passengers.

Instead of reacting in surprise and anger at the actions of other motorists, take things in your stride. Exclamations of anger only mean you have been taken by surprise and are at fault yourself.

By adopting VIP protection attitudes and techniques for everyday driving, you learn to expect the unexpected. You can anticipate any situation and be ready to react. The best way is never to trust any other road user.

Take responsibility for yourself.

Is it not the case that if you feel inclined to make an exclamation of surprise towards other road users, you have trusted them? You didn't really believe that they were about to cause you a mischief. Such 'exclamations', apart from normal comment and opinion, are anathema to an aware driver.

UNAWARE DRIVER

AWARE DRIVER

When you get used to this way of thinking, you turn 'how you used to drive' on its head.

Do it Yourself

Now it is your turn. The next time you get into your car to drive anywhere, set yourself this objective. Drive in a calm, controlled manner avoiding any fancy flourishes; there is no need for fuss. What you are aiming to do is to keep actual and potential dangers in mind and keep yourself in a safe position.

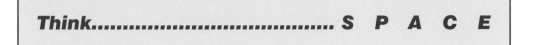

Think... S P A C E

Watch any top class craftsmen or artists at work and you will notice that they have an ability to make what they do look effortless. They have a comfortable economy of movement, a certain grace. They have a vision of what they want to achieve and have the time to do it.

Football fans see these attributes in top class footballers. They instinctively create space and time for themselves and play in it. World-class football players know exactly where to be on the field and are always in the right place at the right time with the minimum of fuss. They are always ahead of the game.

It is exactly the same in other sports; snooker players are always thinking several shots ahead. How do they get so good? Through hours of training, practice and thought about their respective arts.

Being ahead of the game is crucial when it comes to driving too. It is a craft that can be developed and honed.

One of the key qualities that will help a driver with the correct attitude to stand out from the crowd is:

'SMOOOOOTHNESS'

Becoming a smooth operator is your next challenge. To do this you need:

1. A good aware ATTITUDE.
2. To extend OBSERVATIONS.
3. A formulated DRIVING PLAN.

These attributes and how to achieve them will be revealed in the following sections.

What to look for

Your journey to becoming a better driver is now underway.

Awareness and attitude are crucial, but so too is making use of what you can see, your observations, and developing a good acceleration sense.

Observations about observation

Think back to when you were first taught to drive. Your instructor probably emphasised the importance of observation. If you have attended any kind of driving course since passing your test, the emphasis will have been placed on observation.

You are well into this book now and this is the first real mention of observations. Does this strike you as strange? It should, because it is clearly an important consideration. Everybody says so.

This book differs from other books by placing the emphasis on an aware attitude. To understand this, ask yourself; 'What is the point of being able to see something if you do not recognise what is going to kill you?'

Put simply, you have to know what you are looking for and recognise what you see.

When you do, making extended observations is a crucial part of being a good driver. Despite the emphasis in conventional training, it remains one of the biggest failings with the majority of people behind a wheel.

The golden rule is to look as far ahead as possible. It is one thing knowing this rule but it is quite another understanding why it is important.

Firstly, looking ahead gives you time to evaluate what is happening and anticipate what might happen. It enables you to drive in as much available space as possible.

The average motorist looks no more than 25 metres ahead when driving in town and between 100-150 metres ahead when on an open road. If you look into the distance, you will automatically register what is in the foreground, whereas if you look just 25 metres ahead, that is all you will see. Looking ahead enables you to keep everything smooth and simple.

Extend your observations to the top of this hill, looking as far ahead as possible, and you will see a white vehicle just over the crest. Your eyes are designed in such a way that when you look a long way ahead, you also see what is in the foreground, whereas if you look at the vehicle immediately in front of you, that is all you will see.

Notice that you can only see a long way ahead because you are following the preceding vehicle with a minimum two-second gap, a subject covered later in this book.

We have already mentioned that you should try to be smooth when driving and one way to do this is to drive in as straight a line as possible. Looking well ahead helps you to do this.

Drivers who constantly swerve or twitch the steering wheel in order to deal with hazards, except in rare emergency situations, reflect both a poor attitude of awareness and of observation; they are the ones who do not look much further than the front end of their vehicle.

If you are aware of everything that is happening around you, it means you are able to stay in control of the situation. You will give off an aura of calm and you will be able to modify your position on the road gradually.

Before we move on let us cover other driver and driving aspects, all linked to awareness.

Eyesight problems and attitudes

The aware driver's attitude must be 'I have NOT been seen by this driver' and if the vehicle does not pull out into your path, it's only a bonus. To believe that you have been seen is to assume that you have been seen, which is particularly dangerous when you are travelling on a motor cycle.

Rule 81 in the Highway Code (Revised edition 2004) states:

Vision. You **MUST** be able to read a vehicle number plate from a distance of 20.5 metres (67 feet - about five car lengths) in good daylight. From September 2001, you **MUST** be able to read a new style number plate from a distance of 20 metres (66 feet). If you need to wear glasses (or contact lenses) to do this, you **MUST** wear them at all times whilst driving. The police have the power to require a driver, at any time, to undertake an eyesight test in good daylight.

If the police were to conduct roadside eyesight tests, the results would show that numerous drivers would fail this minimum requirement, as many motorists drive without using their necessary or prescribed visual aids.

There are over 30 million drivers in the UK; therefore some hundreds of thousands of them are regularly breaking the law. Think about this statistic next time you see a situation similar to the one in the photograph above, where the driver's head is turned towards you.

Furthermore, let's think about this; where is the logic in requiring drivers to read a number plate at these short distances (a distance only slightly longer than the distance between the wickets on a cricket pitch) and then allowing them to legally drive at 70 mph which equates to travelling at 105 feet (32.3 metres) per second?

Remember, there is no consolation in being 'in the right' and dead.

Acceleration sense

Acceleration Sense is the term developed to describe the ability needed to control the speed of a vehicle by the precise use of the accelerator to meet various traffic conditions. This does not just mean high speeds. 10 mph can be too fast in certain situations. Acceleration Sense comes about when you match your speed to the conditions. It will become second nature, a good habit that you can rely on.

SECTION 3

Anyone can drive too fast

To keep driving as simple as possible, next time you are behind the wheel of your vehicle, give yourself this simple objective; drive as far as possible, especially on a motorway, without using your brake pedal. Clearly you will use your brakes if you think it's necessary, but if you try not to use them, it will ensure two excellent driver attitudes and techniques. You will be looking as far ahead as possible and you will have to keep a good aware 'following distance' (discussed later) behind a preceding vehicle.

This is another clear example of sorting out the mind so that the physical driving skills can look after themselves.

Driving plans

The ability to form a fully assessed driving plan is what separates good drivers from the rest. **Failing to plan is planning to fail.**

Knowing your route and your final destination does not constitute a driving plan. Neither does knowing how to beat the rush hour traffic by choosing to drive down side streets. There is more to it than that. You need to be able to plan your actions throughout your journey, be constantly aware of what is happening around you and be aware of what may happen. All this is achieved by developing good driver habits.

Average drivers do not plan; they only drive on the basis of what they can see. They see something then react; they brake, swerve and shout. Not much of a plan is it?

Watch the average driver following a bus. He drives along without a thought of what the bus is about to do. When it slows down and stops at a bus stop, Mr Average suddenly discovers he is too close. Mr Average then finds that for some unknown reason he has no view beyond the bus. Despite this handicap he decides to take a chance and try to pass it.

Large Goods Vehicle drivers will know what we mean about a lack of planning and the risks people take. They have to be on their guard constantly when driving along country roads because of Mr Average and his love of hogging the whole road and overtaking on blind bends.

Mr Average never gives any thought to what might be around the bend until he actually sees it.

It is not just large vehicles that lead to these potentially dangerous scenarios, there's also the weather. In fog, untrained drivers only see the fog, and do not think about what it may be obscuring.

It's not just the wagon that needs your attention; it's the untrained driver behind it. 'The Lurker.'

Many drivers have been seriously injured or killed in head-on collisions because they have failed to appreciate what is hidden behind an approaching large vehicle. These hidden vehicles are known as 'Lurkers.'

There is no point in getting upset with them. 'Lurker' drivers have never been shown how to overtake correctly. The best they can manage is to suddenly swoop out into the path of oncoming vehicles and take chances. Aware drivers don't take chances; they see opportunities based upon their driver awareness, extended observations and a complete driving plan.

You will find that when unaware drivers make the decision to pull out and overtake, they seldom change their minds. Their original decision is final. They are going to go if it's the last thing they do, and sadly, it often is. If you find yourself driving towards them you will have to make an instant decision to avoid serious consequences. It is no good shouting and hurling abuse at this oncoming driver. If your attitude is to always expect such behaviour, when it happens, you will be able to deal with it effectively and stay alive.

If faced with this situation, you may find that your only safe way out is to drive through a hedge and into a field. The fact that no one may believe you, and they may even laugh at you when you explain what happened, does not matter. You will at least be alive, and all because you were ahead of the game.

Getting angry because of the unexpected actions of Mr Average or Mr Lurker is to be unaware and negative.

If you drive with the correct attitude you make a mental plan, your driving plan, both for what you can see and for what you cannot see. That way you are never taken by surprise. You have to constantly assess three key elements:

1. **What can be seen (the whole of the road in front, behind and to the side).**
2. **What cannot be seen (zones of invisibility – see page 148).**
3. **The circumstances reasonably expected to develop, i.e. 'what if?'**

There are many zones of invisibility. An aware driver remembers the phrase, 'If there's ever a doubt; stay out.'

It is impossible to base all decisions solely on what can be seen. There are many stretches of road where the layout, the weather, traffic conditions, or a combination of them all, do not permit an unobstructed view.

As previously mentioned, an aware driver always considers the 'what if?' factor.

You face your greatest difficulties in areas where the view ahead is blocked by a bend, a corner, a building, the weather conditions or other vehicles.

That is why these three elements are crucial. Whatever the driving conditions, whatever you can see, you have to take into account what cannot be seen and what is likely to develop. It is common sense, but common sense is not all that common.

If you keep all three elements in mind when you are driving, you will have a plan. This planning soon becomes part of the whole driving experience and very quickly you will find that you are not even conscious of formulating your plan. You do it out of habit.

Everyday scenarios

With planning and the correct attitude in mind, take a look at these everyday scenarios. You should begin to see them in a different light. For Mr Average, what you see is what you get; for a driver with the correct attitude, there is much more to it.

How does the aware driver think when...? (Answers on pages 146 to 160)

1 A traffic light is showing 'green' in your favour.

2 A traffic light is showing 'red' against you.

3 You are approaching a zone of invisibility.

4 You are following a moving bus.

5 You are approaching a stationary bus.

6 You are approaching a right-hand bend.

7 You are approaching a left-hand bend.

8 You are approaching a left-hand bend, but a vehicle is parked on your offside just prior to the bend.

9 You are approaching parked vehicles on your near side.

10 You are approaching parked vehicles on your near side, but some of them may be on the 'wrong side' of the road, facing you.

11 You are approaching a pedal cyclist.

12 You are driving along a country lane.

13 You are driving when it starts to rain for the first time in two weeks.

14 You are waiting in a side road in order to join a main road. A vehicle coming from your right, on the main road, has its left-turn indicator flashing.

These might seem straightforward everyday situations, but there is a lot more to think about than you realise. To help guide you through your journey, here are some memory aids to make sure you get it right.

Aware Drivers NEVER Assume

If there is one major problem with today's drivers, it is that they assume and as a result, often get themselves into difficulty.

- They assume that the green traffic light will remain on green.

- They assume that the child or elderly person will remain on the footpath.

- They assume the driver waiting in the side road has seen the vehicle(s) approaching them on the main road.

- They assume that a left indicator means that the vehicle is going to turn left.

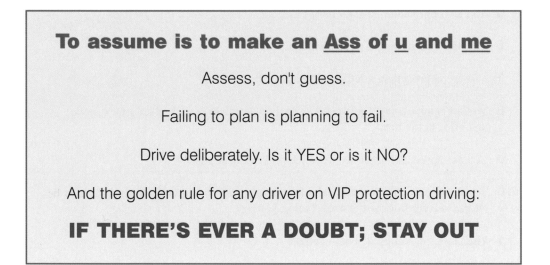

To assume is to make an <u>Ass</u> of <u>u</u> and <u>me</u>

Assess, don't guess.

Failing to plan is planning to fail.

Drive deliberately. Is it YES or is it NO?

And the golden rule for any driver on VIP protection driving:

IF THERE'S EVER A DOUBT; STAY OUT

Time for a change

This book is not about improving your physical driving skills, so why include a section on gear changing? It is here because there are quite a number of aspects of gear changing which relate directly to driver awareness and will help to keep you and your vehicle out of trouble in the event of a sudden emergency.

This advice is aimed towards car drivers who use the average manual gearbox as opposed to drivers of heavier motor vehicles where gearbox design is radically different. Try to put the following into practice so that they become the habits of a driver with the correct attitude.

Finding third

When the gear lever is in the neutral position, you will notice that by pushing the lever either to the right or left, it returns by a spring-loaded mechanism, directly opposite the pathway to third gear. Therefore, third gear is the easiest to obtain from neutral and many drivers are not aware of this. They have a habit of holding the top of the gear lever and moving it around (perhaps looking for 'first' gear for instance, when emerging from a side road onto a main road). Because it is very easy to select third gear instead of first when using this 'chance' method, many drivers stall their engines when moving off from rest.

To eliminate this, develop the habit of holding the gear lever side on, with the palm of your hand facing the direction of the gear you wish to select. In other words, try to create the habit of swivelling your wrist instead of just holding on to the top of the gear lever and taking chances.

The palm pilot

Drivers make too much use of the gear lever, particularly when slowing down or stopping. It is not necessary. The modern gearbox is a wonderful piece of engineering. Try approaching a stationary queue with your vehicle in motion, and as an aware and deliberate driver, you will notice that you can leave the gear lever alone and come to a halt in the queue without either the vehicle 'juddering' to a stop or the driver having to coast the vehicle by early depression of the clutch pedal. Try it.

Remember, the aware driver makes driving look as simple as possible. Some people seem to think the reverse is true. There are drivers who, when they are coming to a halt, change down from 'fifth', to 'fourth', 'third', 'second' and then 'first.'
It is both hard work and unnecessary. Just remember the following:

> ## Brakes to slow, gears to go

There are exceptions, and three of them are listed overleaf.

A lower gear is often an advantage when:
1. Descending steep and winding hills.
2. You are approaching any doubtful road or traffic conditions ahead.
3. Before entry into a hazardous situation (rather than in the middle of one).

Steering

Whenever you change gear, you only have one hand on the steering wheel. For that brief moment the vehicle is not as controlled as it would be if you had two hands on the steering wheel. Both hands should always be on the steering wheel when the vehicle is in a vulnerable position. Therefore:

- If possible, try to avoid changing gear and moving the steering wheel at the same time.

- If possible, try to avoid changing gear alongside a vehicle you are in the process of overtaking. (Especially left hand drive vehicles, because the driver cannot easily see you).

- If possible, try to avoid changing gear on the immediate approach, or almost opposite, an oncoming moving vehicle.

Don't rush

Rushed hand and foot movements will not make the vehicle travel any faster, so avoid rushing your hand and foot movements when changing gear. When moving the gear lever between one gear and another, just try a slight pause with your hand movement whilst the gear lever moves through the neutral position.

Parking gears

When parking, always leave your vehicle in a low gear position. This provides a back-up system for a vehicle handbrake, which may not have been applied properly. There will be no wear and tear on the gearbox by leaving the vehicle in gear (this includes automatic gearboxes). For this reason, it makes sense to get into the habit of depressing the clutch pedal whilst starting the engine. This eliminates the possibility of the vehicle moving forwards (or backwards) when the starter motor is engaged and there is less load placed on the vehicle battery whilst the engine is being started.

Seat belts

Over the years, the compulsory wearing of seat belts has saved many lives and prevented thousands of serious injuries.

If you are one of those motorists who break the law by not wearing a seat belt (other than when manoeuvring and medically exempt), please realise this:

If you don't wear your seat belt, you are at far greater risk of death and injury and also technically uninsured.

Think about that.

How aware are you?

Now you know why awareness is such an important addition to your everyday driving ability, you can continue the journey that will help to transform you into an aware driver.

You have learned not to trust other road users. You can now focus on practical tips that will help every time you drive a vehicle. You can focus on awareness in general, positioning on the road and how to follow other vehicles.

All the driving tips mentioned in the following sections have one thing in common;

S P A C E

There is a lot to take on board, but to make things easy, try to bring some new element of the guidance within this book with you every time you start a journey.

Soon you will be doing it automatically.

General awareness advice

This driving philosophy will probably mean learning to think about the whole business of driving in a new way. Here are some tips to help you to deal with everyday situations.

Parked cars: When passing parked vehicles, leave a gap of at least four feet (a door's width). You never know, a door might open in front of you, a child or elderly person may walk into the roadway from behind a parked vehicle, or the driver of a parked vehicle may start to drive away without proper observations.

Be especially careful if the parked vehicle has two wheels on the footpath. The door is more likely to open to its full extent because of gravity.

If you are unable to keep a four-foot gap, SLOW DOWN, be prepared to stop and give way to oncoming vehicles. Anyone can see a narrow gap and go for it. Aware drivers always ask themselves, 'what if?'

Parking your vehicle

Before parking your vehicle, ask yourself the following simple questions:

Is it SAFE?   Is it CONVENIENT?   Is it LAWFUL?

> *Think of the word 'SKILL.' (SCL). If you can remember these three headings, you will have covered everything the Highway Code has to say on the subject*

Leaving your vehicle

Once parked, you are going to walk away from your vehicle, but remember these points before you do:

- Switch off all auxiliaries before stopping the engine.

- Leave the gear lever in a low gear (first or reverse). This will compliment the handbrake and prevent the vehicle from moving should the handbrake fail.

- If your vehicle has an automatic gear box then move the gearshift into 'P' or Park.

- Ensure that all the doors and windows are locked and secured, making sure that all valuables are out of sight. Look back and check your vehicle as you walk away.

Parking on a car park

In general, try to leave your vehicle in an 'open' space where there are no other vehicles next to it. It is best to leave your vehicle facing outwards so that when you leave, you don't have to reverse out of a space where your view may be obstructed.

If the only available spaces are next to other vehicles and you have to reverse into or out of a space, it is safer to reverse into one. If you leave yourself in a position where you have to reverse out, it is harder to see what is around you because of the other parked vehicles.

If there is a choice of spaces to reverse into, choose a space on your right, you will gain a better view into it as you reverse. You should use this principle if you are driving a van and need to turn the vehicle around to drive in the opposite direction.

When you get into the habit of leaving your vehicle in a space on a car park with no other vehicles around it, you will notice a strange quirk of human nature. Inevitably when you return to your vehicle you will find it surrounded by other vehicles. It happens on supermarket car parks as well as motorway service stations. Even when there are other more convenient spaces, people tend to show a kind of herding instinct.

Whenever you return to your vehicle and it has been out of your sight for some time, always check for damage. It is better to know where the damage occurred rather than to find it later.

Moving off

Before moving off, consider turning on all the driving auxiliaries you require, wipers, lights, and so on. You should check that you have enough fuel for your journey. It will save you having to refuel when you are travelling. When you are ready to drive away, take a good look all around and especially over your shoulder.

Temporary stops: If you are driving along in a normal traffic flow and come to a temporary stop and you anticipate that the stop will be longer than three seconds, apply the handbrake immediately. Vehicle stability is required and it is not a good idea to wear out the clutch mechanism or to distract the driver to your rear who is faced with your bright rear braking lights.

Signals: Give signals clearly and in good time. Do not forget that one of the most important signals is the courtesy signal. If someone affords you a right of way, it is only good manners to say 'Thank You', even if the other driver had no other choice.

Other drivers' courtesy: Always be wary if another driver indicates for you to proceed either by hand, horn or lights. They may not see the complete situation or worse still, they could wave you into danger out of mischief. Consider that there may be a cyclist or motorcyclist travelling along either side of the queue. Courtesy should always be acknowledged, but you should make your own decisions with regard to committing yourself to a particular action or manoeuvre.

Aware drivers don't trust anyone

Question: Showing courtesy towards other road users is a major factor towards safe driving and is not annoying to other drivers. It's called good manners.

Why then, is there no mention in the Highway Code of a courtesy signal when someone gives way to you?

Emerging from a junction

When you are on a side road waiting to join the traffic on the main road, you must always give way. There are times when the traffic flow is so heavy that it is impossible to find a gap in the traffic to move into.

Whilst waiting to emerge from a junction you can use mind-games. Wind your drivers' door window down and look at drivers on the main road in the eye. Don't look through glass, or sun glasses. Try it. 99 times out of 100, you will find that the driver on the main road will allow you out of your junction. However, you must still use your own judgement and not just emerge because the other driver allows you to do so. Make your own mind up and think about the 'what if?' factor, looking especially for a motorbike rider or cyclist. Don't forget to give the considerate driver a courtesy signal.

Traffic light junctions

In your mind's eye, think of all traffic light junctions as having yellow boxes painted on the road surface. Do not enter the junction unless it is safe to do so and your exit is clear. Aware drivers do not need painted yellow boxes.

Yellow Box junction with yellow paint.

'Yellow Box' junction without yellow paint

The exception to the rule is if you are turning right but are prevented from doing so by oncoming traffic. Always move well into the junction if you are intending to turn right.

If you are approaching a set of lights showing a green light in your favour, look into the opposing junction on your approach to ensure your passage is clear. Do not assume it is safe to proceed simply because your traffic light shows green.

Finally, remember that a red light is not a physical barrier and cannot prevent another vehicle from driving through it. With that in mind, even when your signal is green, check that other drivers are not putting you and your passengers in danger by driving through a light on red. You only have one life. What consolation is there in being in the right if you are dead or seriously injured?

Slippery road surfaces: Care has to be taken on slippery surfaces, but do not think that this category simply includes ice and snow. When it rains, road surfaces become hazardous. Engine and gearbox oil, diesel and tyres, all leave their residue on roads, and when they mix with water, all the ingredients exist for an efficient skidpan.

The four main causes of skids are:
- Excessive speed for the existing conditions.
- Coarse steering in relation to a speed, which in itself is not excessive.
- Harsh acceleration.
- Excessive or sudden braking.

The Correct Speed: Knowing the correct speed for the current conditions is crucial. The correct speed is not a question of how fast you can get from A to B, but how quickly you can react to a situation and stop.

Take a look at your speedometer and note the speed at which you are travelling. When you add half as much again to your speed in miles per hour, you will discover how many feet per second your vehicle is travelling at.

For example,
30 mph = (30+15) 45 feet per second
70 mph = (70+35) 105 feet per second

No matter how hard you concentrate, it takes at least two thirds of a second to react before taking any action. That is your thinking distance. At 70 mph this equates to some 70 feet. In other words, at 70 mph you will travel 70 feet before either braking or steering (63 mph = 63 feet etc).

Think about this the next time you see a vehicle 'slipstreaming' another vehicle on a motorway. You will then understand why the majority of crashes on main roads are rear end collisions.

These distances only apply if you are physically and mentally fit, have good eyesight and are not on prescribed medication or drugs that could affect your driving and concentration. If you are reading a map, talking on a hand held mobile phone (which is illegal and places you in a position where you are unable to fully control your vehicle), chatting with a passenger or changing a CD etc., you are affecting the time you have available to react.

Dual carriageways

You will need to have had experience in the police to know just how many motorists travel the wrong way on dual carriageways.

The offence, or action, is usually (but not always) committed during the evening or night-time. It's usually committed by people who haven't been concentrating on their driving (although criminal activity is also sometimes involved). Nevertheless, driving in the opposite direction on dual carriageways is quite a common occurrence.

The question is simple. Where is the consolation in becoming involved with a vehicle travelling the wrong way on a dual carriageway and then saying, 'it wasn't my fault'? There's no consolation whatsoever.

It's far better not to become involved in the first place and if you now believe just what a common occurrence it is, the next time you observe such a vehicle WHEN it happens, you will be much more likely to deal with it and less likely to become involved.

Please remember, 'nothing surprises the aware driver' and if you ever find yourself making exclamations of surprise towards other motorists, you will be trusting them. Such trust is anathema to an aware driver.

Roundabouts

Roundabouts can be a major source of worry for the average driver. They do not know how to treat them.

It is simple. Roundabouts are just another name for crossroads and their purpose is to make a one-way traffic flow and help vehicles on the move.

There is always diesel, oil and rubber on the road at the approach to any roundabout. Never assume that the driver ahead of you will move off, or continue to enter the roundabout, even when the road is clear.

When following another vehicle on the approach to a roundabout, which is clear of traffic, expect the driver of that vehicle to stop or slow down for no apparent reason. The majority of drivers do not look to their right until they actually arrive at the roundabout junction. Many crashes at roundabouts are rear-end shunts.

Do not consider pulling alongside a long vehicle at a roundabout.

Drivers of long vehicles often position themselves in the near side lane to make the negotiation of the roundabout easier but will encroach into the offside lane as they go around it.

Alongside a long vehicle carrying out this manoeuvre is not somewhere you, as an aware driver, want to be.

General tips on roundabouts:

Read the advance direction sign carefully and think of the roundabout as a clock face. Count the number of exits, including your own, and count them again as you are negotiating the roundabout.

If your exit on the roundabout is the first left turn then it should be dealt with as a normal left turn.

If your exit on the roundabout is beyond 'twelve o'clock' then it should be dealt with as a normal right turn.

If you intend to go straight ahead (at approximately the twelve o'clock position shown on the sign) then no signal is required until you are in the position as described in the next paragraph.

When leaving a roundabout, all junctions are a left turn. A left signal should be considered when you are alongside the exit immediately before the one you intend to take.

Immediately before leaving the roundabout it is highly recommended that you look over your shoulders to check that your vehicle is clear of hazards.

Positioning

The best way to understand positioning is to think of your vehicle as being within an imaginary glass bubble. Your job is to keep the vehicle in a safe position while you negotiate both the actual and potential dangers.

There are three types of hazard that present danger:

● Physical features i.e. junctions, bends, hills, roundabouts etc.
● Those created by other road users.
● Road and weather conditions.

Dealing with hazards is simple. On the approach to them, you have to consider your options:

1. Course (Plan it early).
2. Signal (Do I need to give one?).
3. Speed (To negotiate the hazard safely).
4. Gear (To control the speed).

The Three 'V's

When approaching a roundabout, instead of just changing down, fifth to fourth, to third, to second and then stopping to engage first, assess the following before you select the appropriate gear. It makes your driving life a lot simpler. Remember that an aware driver always makes it look easy.

● **V**EHICLES (Those approaching and already on the roundabout).

● **V**IEW (Into the roundabout).

● CUR**V**E (How severe is the bend?).

Following other vehicles

Following other vehicles is the norm for at least 90 per cent of your time behind the wheel. When you are following another vehicle there is one golden rule to keep in mind.

> ## Only a fool
> ## breaks the 'Two-Second' rule

Look at these two pictures. They are both horror stories.

Where is your extended view in front of this preceding vehicle?
How could you possibly stop safely if this driver applied his brakes?
How could you extend your braking distance for a 'tailgater' to your rear?
How can you see, and make a full assessment of the road ahead?

In other words, to get yourself into a position like these pictures show is to put your vehicle, and your life, into the hands of the untrained driver.

Applying the 'Two-Second' rule is easy. Watch the vehicle in front of you pass any point or feature on the roadway and say 'Only a fool breaks the 'Two-Second' rule' out loud. If you pass that point before you finish speaking, then you are too close for safety.

Remember what you have learned so far. There is a high probability that the driver in front of you is unskilled and unaware. If your driver attitude isn't correct, you may be lead into a dangerous situation from which there is no easy way out.

This 'Two-Second' rule has to be regarded as an absolute minimum and in the case of poor road conditions or bad weather, you should double it. When you create a space in front of you, another driver might cut into that space. If so, he is putting himself in danger, not you. Simply drop back and create you own space again.

There are a number of advantages that following someone at a correct distance gives to the driver with the correct attitude:

- You are able to see more, both in the immediate vicinity and in the distance.
- You can stop safely if the driver in front suddenly applies his brakes without warning.
- You can extend your own braking distance into the gap in front of you so that anyone following you too closely is given more time to react.
- You can overtake in as straight a line as possible when the opportunity arises.

What if the traffic is stopped? What is the minimum distance you should keep between yourself and the vehicle in front of you?

In this common situation, the best rule to remember is:

Keep sight of 'T on T' (Tyres on the Tarmac)

This means that you should leave enough room so that you can see the rear wheels of the vehicle in front of you; you can see 'tyres on the tarmac.'

This will give you enough time and space to react if the vehicle in front rolls back on a hill or the driver accidentally selects reverse instead of a forward gear.

Finally, if the vehicle in front breaks down, you will have room in which to manoeuvre around it. The same goes in the unlikely event of someone personally attacking you or your vehicle in the queue.

Remember, always take responsibility for yourself

Making your moves

Now is the time to take a closer look at some of the key manoeuvres: overtaking, cornering and reversing.

Overtaking

You are in traffic, in space and in control. The vehicle directly in front is a slower one and you want to get past it. You are at the point when you are looking to overtake.

There are many places where it is illegal to overtake and you will be familiar with these, so we will not go into detail here.

Even where it is a perfectly legitimate act, overtaking is one of the most dangerous manoeuvres you are likely to perform. It calls for planning.

Planning in this case means that when you approach another vehicle from the rear and anticipate having to overtake it, you look for an early opportunity.

If that opportunity does not arise, adopt the 'Following Position' as discussed earlier, remembering the 'Two-Second' rule.

> ## Look for an opportunity, not a chance.
> ## A chance is a gamble

Look at the pictures opposite.

Obtain your own view. Don't take chances; only opportunities.

Don't overtake in an arc. The first move, having obtained your own view, is to move sideways to confirm a clear road ahead. If you overtake on an arc, get alongside the overtaken vehicle and then become unsure, you have lost your **s p a c e** and your life is at risk.

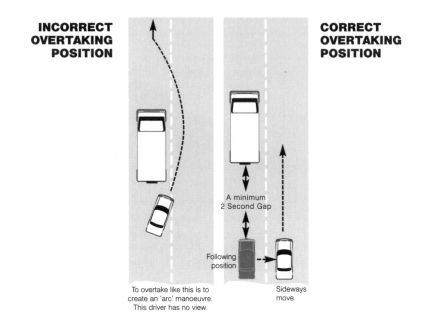

INCORRECT OVERTAKING POSITION

CORRECT OVERTAKING POSITION

A minimum
2 Second Gap

Following
position

To overtake like this is to
create an 'arc' manoeuvre.
This driver has no view.

Sideways
move

There are three things to keep in mind when you are overtaking which will help you and your fellow road users:

● Never cause the vehicle you are overtaking to have to change course or speed.

● Try to avoid becoming a third line of vehicles travelling abreast, either in the same or opposite directions.

● Always leave yourself time to move back to your near side.

● Remember that the faster you travel during the 'overtake', the faster you are approaching an oncoming vehicle. That is why good acceleration sense is essential.

The act of overtaking means that you will have to make a number of important assessments. You need to judge the speed of the vehicles you wish to overtake, relative to the speed and performance of your own vehicle, and ask yourself if you have got the power and acceleration required to carry out the manoeuvre.

You need to assess the speed of approaching vehicles that are in view and as you should be aware by now, the likely speed of approaching vehicles that you cannot see.

Another key consideration is the distance available to overtake and regain your position towards the near side.

Finally, you have to look out for any road junctions or obstructions that may lie ahead, as there may be cars at or approaching them and the drivers may not see you. Only when you are happy that these critical assessments have been made can you consider going ahead with the overtaking manoeuvre.

Making these assessments will then make overtaking a straightforward manoeuvre. It is only the unaware driver who makes it complicated. Here are some guidelines based on the results of overtaking manoeuvres that did not work.

NEVER start to overtake unless you have made a full assessment and have identified somewhere for your vehicle to go both during and at the end of your manoeuvre.

NEVER commit yourself to an overtaking manoeuvre from behind another vehicle without first obtaining a full view of the road ahead.

NEVER follow another vehicle through an overtaking manoeuvre. Make your own decisions. Remember, an aware driver NEVER trusts another road user.

NEVER carry out an overtaking manoeuvre in the line of an arc. (See diagram)

Always be looking to give yourself somewhere to go for additional safety, it is called **S P A C E** . That is why making a full assessment of all the circumstances is vital.

Overtaking does not have to be difficult. You can simplify the whole process.

It is a question of attitude, observation, planning and acceleration sense. When you consider observation, check the view on both sides of the vehicle you want to overtake. Check the views in your mirrors and act on both what you can and cannot see.

Overtaking Simplified

View – Mirror – Out – Confirm – Go

OR

Return to the nearside – into the S P A C E at the side of you

DO NOT OVERTAKE IN AN ARC

When you want to get into position for overtaking, move out sideways, not out and forward. You will then be in a position to see the road ahead and confirm your action; yes, no or hold back.

Once you have decided it is safe to overtake, proceed positively in a straight line, parallel to the vehicle you are passing and leaving a minimum six-foot space (side-on) between the two vehicles.

It is that simple. However, there are more things for the thinking driver to be aware of.

For instance:
- Do not forget Mr Lurker.
- Be careful on the approach to junctions.
- If you are overtaking two or three vehicles at once, be aware that one of these may see the same opportunity as you and move out into your path.

OVERTAKING EXAMPLE, see pictures opposite:

(TOP) Before overtaking any left hand drive vehicle, remember the driver may not be able to see you alongside, neither by using his mirrors nor looking out of the side window.

(BOTTOM) All overtaking should be fully assessed and deliberate.When you have completed the overtaking manoeuvre, do not cut in ahead of the other driver. Leave plenty of room. Remember planning, courtesy and smoothness.You should NEVER cause the vehicle you overtake to have to alter course or speed.

Going round the bend

There is a basic technique when driving round corners and bends, which is designed to make the job easier for you and your vehicle.

All corners should be treated as hazards and knowing this, you have to treat them with respect. Always consider your course, speed and gear on your approach to them, not when you arrive at them. By then, it can be too late.

Your objective with corners is to negotiate them at a constant speed. This will give you the required control of your vehicle.

It is all a matter of basic physics. A vehicle travelling at a constant speed around a curve is relatively stable because the weight of the vehicle is partially transferred to the rear.

By becoming flatter to the road surface, the rear tyres will have a better grip.

Consequently, because the weight of the vehicle is transferred to the rear, the steering will become lighter. This applies to both front-wheel drive and four-wheel drive vehicles.

Look at the opposite scenario. When a vehicle is travelling around a curve under deceleration, or under braking, the opposite will occur; the weight will be transferred onto the front wheels and that will make the steering heavier. The vehicle will become more unstable.

The other point about corners is that they limit your view.   Do not drive simply on what you can see. Think about what you cannot see and what might reasonably be expected to develop.

Always be able to stop well within the distance that you can see is clear and do not ignore the possibility of a moving vehicle or stationary obstruction around the bend in a zone of invisibility.

Let's think about this. In a government publication, in the section about cornering, it states that a driver should be 'able to stop in the distance seen to be clear.' Here then, is a picture of the same bend taken from opposite directions. If you should be 'able to stop in the distance seen to be clear,' then what would happen if you were faced with a moving vehicle occupying the whole of the road? Point A in the top picture is the maximum view for you, the driver. Point B in the bottom picture is the maximum view a driver would have of a vehicle coming towards him. Even if each driver saw the other immediately, there would still be a stopping distance to consider, somewhere around point C. Therefore it is not good enough to be 'able to stop in the distance seen to be clear.' At the very least, it should say, 'able to stop well within the distance seen to be clear.' Aware drivers never base their driving plan just on what they can see, they also consider the circumstances reasonably expected to develop.

Positioning

On the approach to a right hand bend, move towards the nearside.

On the approach to a left hand bend, move towards the centre of the road.

There are several reasons why you should adopt this practice.

1. It will improve your view of the road ahead. For every centimetre you modify your position, your view will be increased by metres.

2. On right hand bends, oncoming traffic will be furthest away as those drivers negotiate the curve of the bend.

3. The turning circle of the vehicle will be increased, which enhances the vehicle's stability.

4. You should always aim to keep the turning circle as large as possible and drive close to the apex of the bend. This reduces the effects of centrifugal force.

As an aware driver, the correct position on the approach to a bend is an essential habit to adopt. It will quickly become second nature.

Reversing

As a general rule, do not be afraid to ask for help. If you are unable to see fully, seek assistance. Do not let your ego result in a crash.

One obvious point. Be especially aware when reversing in car parks. Other vehicles and pedestrians use them and they will be coming at you from all directions. You also need to look for low walls, posts and motorcycles etc.. When in doubt, get out of the vehicle and take a look around.

How to reverse into a gap between parked vehicles on a road (on your nearside).

1. The gap between the other parked vehicles should be at least one and a half times the length of your vehicle.

2. Drive well forward of the gap, keeping a space of one metre from the side of the front vehicle.

3. Ensure that there is no moving traffic around and reverse into the gap keeping the same one metre space between you and the front vehicle.

4. Looking from the driver's seat, line up the centre of your rear windscreen with an imaginary mark on the footpath or kerb edge, showing the second third of the available space. When the vehicle is at the correct angle, straighten the wheels.

5. Keep your speed slow but constant.

6. When the front of your vehicle has passed the rear offside corner of the front vehicle, apply right-hand steering-lock, smoothly and gradually, and then straighten up your vehicle with the kerb edge.

7. Park close and parallel to the kerb (within six inches if possible). If there are shop windows at the roadside, use them as a visual aid. They reflect images and can be a great help.

Motorway Driving

'During a practical demonstration, it will take a good teacher at least one and a half hours to mention, just once, everything there is to know about motorway driving; laws, regulations, attitudes and techniques.

Then extra time will be required to elaborate and briefly discuss this information.

If you have ever received information about driving on a motorway and you haven't been given at least one and a half hours of non-repetitive information, then you have been short changed.'

The Basics

Look at an average motorway and what do you see? Cars, vans, buses, trucks and motorcycles. Blurs on black tarmac.

Now think about the bigger picture. It was established earlier that you should consider every other vehicle on the road as being driven by someone who, because they were never taught properly how to drive on motorways, is unskilled and unaware. Think again about the average motorway scene.

Most drivers on a motorway see cars, vans and trucks, whereas aware drivers see missiles. When you drive on a motorway, you are in the same position as the pilot of an aircraft flying in high-speed formation, except you are now surrounded by untrained strangers; a very dangerous activity.

Motorways are often described as boring. Even the Highway Code (Rule 236) refers to them as monotonous. This is the thinking of unaware and unskilled drivers. In all honesty, how could boredom possibly be a factor on your journey when in essence, you are surrounded by high-speed missiles which are being controlled and guided by unskilled operatives? Most drivers have had little or no tuition on a motorway, yet they would probably describe themselves as experts.

When you drive as an aware driver, in **s p a c e** and trusting no one, you soon realise that motorways can be a great source of entertainment. Statistics show that there are fewer crashes, mile for mile, on motorways than on any other category of road in the country.

The problem is when crashes do happen, they often have tragic consequences. Why? Inappropriate speed is a factor, but the lack of driver education and advice on how to drive on motorways, has everything to do with it.

You can do something about that. Let's get back to basics. Here is a recap of the principles of **MIND HOW YOU GO**.

The main objective is to drive your vehicle in as much available space as possible and to avoid using your brakes unless it is absolutely necessary. To achieve this space, and to avoid unnecessary braking, there are two golden rules:

1. **Look as far ahead as possible.**

2. **Stick to the minimum 'Two-Second' rule when you are following another vehicle.**

Joining a motorway

On the slip road to a motorway, you will see a large blue rectangular sign, which marks the fact that beyond it, motorway regulations will now be in force. These regulations include the national speed limit of 70 mph.

Once you are on the slip road heading on to a motorway, you should be assertive. Be careful when you are following someone else onto a slip road. As far as you are concerned, that driver is unskilled and has had no specific motorway training; they do not know what to do and will have no idea what to do if faced with any kind of obstruction on the road ahead.

If you find yourself following another vehicle down a slip road joining a motorway, always give the preceding driver a lot of space. Remember that other drivers have not generally received any tuition on how to join the motorway. If they encounter a problem, make sure that the problem doesn't involve you.

Therefore, if you are following someone, give them plenty of space. Furthermore, by giving yourself space, you have time to take action and escape should the need arise.

The ideal way to join the main motorway is by using Acceleration Sense. Avoid being too close to someone else and so limit your options.

There is one crucial fact about driving on motorways that you need to know.

Most motorway crashes happen close to junctions and within road works.

You are approaching a junction. This is where drivers will change lanes, slow down and speed up without planning their actions.

Changing lanes should not be a problem to an aware driver, because they are fully aware of the potential problems that surround them.

However, for the unskilled and unthinking driver, changing lanes can lead to big problems. One of the main reasons for their difficulties is the fact that they are unaware and leave their decision too late.

When driving along the nearside lane, be especially aware as you drive either on the immediate approach to, or alongside the slip road leading off the motorway. Quite a number of drivers, especially on busy motorways, leave their exit manoeuvre far too late and cut across drivers who are driving quite normally in the nearside lane. Aware drivers pay special attention to their offside at or near junctions leading off motorways.

Road works present a real problem for all drivers. They cut down the available road space and as you know, space is vital for safety.

There is more to it than that. Slip roads and road works cause problems for unaware drivers because they only act on what they can see immediately in front of them. They do not look into the distance. All they see is the rear of the vehicle in front. This does not leave them enough time to react and negotiate the hazard safely.

How should you differ from the rest? As you already know, it helps to have a driving plan and it helps to be aware of the limitations of the people around you.

Knowing where most accidents occur, take particular care at all junctions and in road works where the road width is restricted.

Being aware that fellow road users are generally unskilled is one thing, but having a plan when they try and harm you is what separates you from them. You constantly need to be aware of having a space into which you can escape.

When travelling along any motorway in this country, you should always be aware of the following:

You are surrounded by missiles, so do not trust any other road users. They do not look as far ahead as you and do not recognise real and potential hazards, nor do they create or maintain reasonable road space.

As an aware driver, expect nothing but trouble from all other road users.

When other road users are behaving themselves, it's only a bonus.

Motorway hazards

There are potential hazards on all roads, but by their very nature, motorways generate some that are specific to them.

The Closing Gap: A Closing Gap occurs when a vehicle ahead is catching up to one travelling in the same lane. This means that the vehicle behind is likely to change lanes in order to overtake. Looking out for the Closing Gap is one of the differences between ordinary missile drivers and aware drivers like you.

The speed of the dark coloured car could create a Closing Gap. See these situations early, and either move out (earlier than this photograph shows) or give way, without timidity.

Looking for Closing Gaps should be one of the good habits you develop. It is not simply a case of looking ahead to the car in front and driving on what you can see. It is taking a view of the whole picture and working out what might happen. Once you understand the idea, it can become a very satisfying part of motorway driving. You will be able to predict which vehicle will switch lanes to overtake long before the thought actually occurs to the driver of that particular vehicle.

An aware driver always makes driving look simple

Knowing what others may do clearly has an effect on your own driving plan. If you are catching up to a vehicle that you believe is about to move out into your lane, you should consider your alternatives. You can move out yourself or you can stay where you are and give way. What you need to avoid is being forced into an unwanted 'last second' manoeuvre. You should be in command of the road and in control of the situation, making decisions for yourself rather than being forced to react to something.

It is vital that you are fully aware of what is going on behind you. The option of changing lanes to allow someone out might not be available to you if there are several vehicles approaching at speed from your rear. In such circumstances, you must be assertive but can still give way to the driver ahead. Assertive does not mean the same as aggressive.

The objective should be to ensure that you are in space, with time on your side.

Don't be bullied. Command the road

There are bullies everywhere in life, but motorways seem to bring out the bully in a lot of people. It is not an attractive trait, but it seems to be human nature to pick on the timid. Timid drivers do get picked on.

The way you drive sends signals out to other road users. If you are positive and deliberate in your actions, you are always in charge, but if you are slow, timid or hesitant, then there will be others ready to take advantage of you, and your problems will increase.

For example, if you spot a Closing Gap and the vehicle ahead appears likely to want to pull into your lane to overtake, the driver would sense any hesitancy from you and see it as a sign of weakness and pull out in front of you, regardless of the consequences.

Giving way to drivers is a good thing, as long as you control the situation. Sometimes it is neither safe nor convenient to give way.

Beware of timidity. Timid drivers are often abused, it's human nature

---

Getting blown off course

Strong side winds are common on long bleak stretches of open roads and can play havoc with traffic on motorways. Strong side winds can blow you off course and across the carriageway.

There is a highly effective technique that will help you to keep your vehicle stable and to counteract the sideways push from Mother Nature.

If you are experiencing such problems, the answer is to very *briefly* take your foot OFF the accelerator pedal.

You are not attempting to slow the vehicle down, because if you do, you may inconvenience traffic behind you. By taking your foot off the accelerator, you will momentarily transfer the weight of your vehicle towards the front, normally towards the engine. You will then have that extra weight on the front wheels to assist your vehicle's stability.

In strong side winds, if you keep your foot on the power, you will make the problem worse. The weight goes towards the rear and it is easier to be blown off course.

It is that simple. This information may not stop a high-sided vehicle from being blown over, but it will reduce the risk.

Changing lanes

Changing lanes can be potentially dangerous; that is why junctions and road works lead to difficulties and crashes. There are certain things you can do to minimise these problems when you want to change lanes.

If possible, avoid positioning yourself directly alongside another vehicle; the other driver may also be looking to change lanes.

Space is important. You should try to avoid travelling with another moving vehicle directly alongside. You need space because you need somewhere to escape to, and having another vehicle alongside you blocks off a possible escape route. Do not allow your options to be limited. Make sure that you have space by using your Acceleration Sense. It can help keep others ahead or behind you.

Most drivers do not look sideways

We know that finding space on heavily congested motorways is sometimes impossible, but the fundamentals; attitude and observations, still apply. You should always be aware and in control.

When you have overtaken a left hand drive truck, do not move into the lane occupied by the truck until you are well clear of the front of it and the driver can see you.

Apply the same thinking in any of the overtaking lanes when you have a vehicle on your immediate left.

The straight-line steer

On many occasions you will be able to change lanes without actually steering.
You simply allow your vehicle to take advantage of the natural curve in the road. To do
this, you have to be looking well ahead. If the road is curving round to the left and you
want to move into the lane on your right, you can often make the move simply by staying
in a straight line. Similarly, when you are on a right hand curve and you wish to move
from one of the outer lanes to the left hand lane, you can do so by using the curve of the
bend.

When you have accomplished the essential habit of looking well ahead, you will see what
little effort is actually required to steer in order to change lanes. This photograph shows a
typical example. It is the bend in the road, which can take you from the nearside lane and
into the centre lane, without having to physically use the steering wheel. Aware drivers
always drive in as straight a line as possible, and this method of changing lanes is known
as a straight-line steer. Remember to signal your intention to any following driver.

The early move is always the wise move

A lack of education leads to most drivers performing high speed, last minute lane switches. They tend to treat motorways just as they do normal roads, but at high speed their technique is found wanting. Unaware drivers can be seen swerving to overtake slower vehicles at the last minute. Others travel far too close to the vehicle in front and are constantly applying the brake. They have no appreciation of relative speeds.

What does making the early move mean in reality? Imagine driving along the nearside lane on a motorway and catching up to a slower vehicle, some way ahead of you and in the same lane. You intend to overtake this vehicle, but if you don't move out early into an overtaking lane, you will find yourself having to slow down because of faster vehicles overtaking from your rear.

When you find yourself in the position of becoming the slower vehicle yourself, your own hazards will have greatly increased. You will have become disadvantaged. That is why making an early move is important.

FACT. Slower drivers on open roads and motorways have more hazards to deal with than faster drivers. This information is not to be regarded as an encouragement to be the faster driver (someone has got to be the slower driver) but that is the way it is.

Fast lane survival

There is no such thing as a 'fast' lane or a 'slow' lane, but on motorways with more than two lanes, drivers in the nearside and middle lanes commonly experience more difficulties than the faster drivers in the outside lane.

This is not surprising. Drivers travelling on the inside lanes have much more to consider. They have vehicles to their front and rear, others filtering from their left at junctions and still more from their right, either in the process of overtaking them, or worse still, cut across drivers at junctions; the offending driver having made a very late move in order to leave the main carriageway of the motorway.

Drivers of vehicles travelling faster in the outside lane generally do not have as many hazards to concern them. Their main considerations are the speed and possible actions of those drivers in front of them and on their left.

It is also a fact that faster drivers tend to apply a greater degree of concentration than slower drivers (See 'Eight Blunders Of The World'). However, this should not be read as a defence for driving too fast.

Recent developments have made life more difficult for vehicles in the nearside lanes.

Following a small number of public service vehicle crashes, legislation now prohibits all buses and coaches, which are designed to carry more than eight seated passengers in addition to the driver, or with a gross weight exceeding 7.5 tonnes, from using the outside lane of motorways with more than two lanes.

As a result, buses and coaches now have to travel among lines of large goods vehicles, many of which carry hazardous loads. On wet road surfaces, these LGVs create large amounts of spray, hampering visibility.

Many coach drivers will tell you that since they are no longer allowed to use the outside lane, LGVs have a tendency to ride in convoy with them, as they do amongst themselves. This puts coach drivers and their passengers at even more risk of a serious collision.

As there is no compulsory driver attitude education or advice for this category of vehicle-driver, the same problem drivers exist. The only difference is that they are commanding even bigger missiles. They have less room in which to manoeuvre than a car driver and still encounter the same problems when travelling too close to the vehicles in front.

Frustration has now been added to their existing attitude problems.

Despite the change in the law, crashes involving buses and coaches still occur on a daily basis.

It is only a matter of time before there will be a serious loss of life caused by a crash on a motorway involving a coach and a goods vehicle carrying a chemical or other hazardous load.

Campaigners back up their decision to slow down buses and coaches by maintaining that **'Speed Kills.'** We believe that this memorable phrase is incomplete. It should read: **'Speed Kills when the wrong people use it in the wrong place'.**

The latter phrase underlines the point that speed in itself is not the issue. Sometimes ten mph can be too fast.

The emergency services travel to incidents as quickly as possible when lives are believed to be in danger. That usually means exceeding the speed limit, but the drivers have been trained how to deal with speed. It is part of their specialist training.

Hazardous loads

We mentioned vehicles carrying hazardous loads on the previous page and it is important for an aware driver to be able to recognise one.

They all have coloured hazard warning plates (as shown). The symbol and number on the sign identify the type of load. There will also be an emergency telephone contact number.

If you see a vehicle like this with its load leaking, spilled, or involved in a crash, you should:

- Keep clear.
- Extinguish naked flames and do not smoke.
- Switch off mobile telephones and other electrical equipment.
- Bring leakage to the attention of the driver.

If you are able to contact the authorities, do so well away from the scene. Make a note of the symbols and numbers on the marking plate. This will identify the spilled substance immediately and give the authorities the information they need to take appropriate action.

Thinking distance

We mentioned the 'Two-Second' rule earlier and covered thinking distances. When you are travelling at high speed, your thinking distance, the distance you travel before reacting to something, is higher. You travel much further before reacting.

The existing advice for motorway drivers is 'Keep Your Distance', a meaningless statement if you haven't been told what that distance is.

'Check your Distance' or 'Keep your Distance.' What's the use of signs like this when, because of the lack of official and proper driver education, no one knows what 'your distance' is? Signs like this are a complete waste of taxpayers' money.

In the days when vehicles were fitted with drum brakes, 'Stopping Distances' were quoted in the Highway Code. These same figures are quoted in the current edition. However, modern vehicles, with improved technology, can now stop in far less distance than they did when those calculations were made. The advice in the Highway Code under 'Typical Stopping Distances' is both out of date and unrealistic. Why do we have signs which say 'Keep Your Distance', when even the Highway Code cannot tell us what that distance now is?

How do you know what a safe distance is at 27, 44, or 68 mph? There is no specific advice available to drivers in general. It is not part of regular driver education.

To add insult to serious and fatal injuries, drivers involved in motorway pile-ups are often labelled as 'idiots' by the authorities. Why are the same drivers not given meaningful training in the first place? At least then if they make a mistake the 'idiot' tag may be justified.

It is a fact that a driver who is fully aware and focusing his attention completely on driving, can bring a modern vehicle to a safe stop in a much shorter distance than the Stopping Distances stated in the Highway Code.

It is also true to say that 'Learner' drivers, inexperienced drivers, drivers with poor eyesight and sleepy drivers (to name but a few), will need at least half as much space again in order to stop their vehicle safely.

There are now white chevrons painted onto the road surface and you are advised to 'Keep Apart Two Chevrons.' Very good; the authorities now want you to drive along the motorway, surrounded by missiles, and drivers who don't know what they are doing, staring at the road surface counting to yourself, 'one-two' 'one-two.'

If there is anything more stupid than that then we have yet to see it. Aware drivers are constantly looking out of their windscreens and into their mirrors to keep themselves as far away from actual and potential dangers as possible. They do not just stare at the road surface.

It is not a case of what you do, it is knowing what to do.

Sadly, these photographs are typical of scenes on British motorways. The driver of the silver car and these wagon drivers are an accident (crash) waiting to happen.

Knowing and applying the phrase 'Only a Fool Breaks The Two-Second Rule' (Rule 105 Highway Code) is a start. There is more to it than that. When you notice a lorry travelling just a few feet behind another lorry, you need to be aware that it would only take a puncture, a small piece of debris or a stray animal to create chaos.

In those situations, you have to be aware of what might happen and remain in space. Be aware of the possible dangers around you.

The 'Two-Second' gap is a minimum. If visibility or the road surface is poor, then you should increase the gap.

It is up to you to take responsibility for yourself and any VIPs you have with you. Whilst we would not call other road users idiots, we will point out a fact to heighten your state of awareness.

You know how to calculate how many feet per second you are travelling. It is your mph multiplied by 1.5. Therefore at 50 mph you travel 75 feet per second; at 70 mph, 105 feet per second and so on.

Some drivers have a habit of turning their head in order to chat to front seat passengers and do not realise they are doing it. At 70 mph, if you look at your passenger for two seconds, you will have driven over 200 feet without looking where you are going. Think about that the next time you are holding a conversation whilst driving.

Other motorway hazards

Debris is a major factor in motorway accidents (crashes). Tyres, wood, wire, rope, sheeting, bricks, stone, exhausts and luggage are some of the things you are likely to find lying in your path on motorway journeys.

Dogs and other animals come into this category. Stray animals on the carriageway are often the reason why the motorway warning signs, advising a lower speed limit, (which most motorists tend to ignore), have been switched on. Loose animals can bring a motorway to a complete standstill. The standing traffic then becomes a major hazard in itself. That is why we class them as debris.

Debris causes a problem because drivers do not see it soon enough and then brake or swerve to avoid it. It is this dramatic late reaction that leads to problems, which can be avoided by extended observation.

At night, debris tends to be less of a problem because drivers do not see it until it is too late to do anything about it. The debris is hit and, whilst there may be some damage to their vehicle, the incident does not involve others.

Tyre troubles

On an average shift, a motorway patrol police officer spends most of his incident time dealing in some way with punctures. Punctures cause accidents. Punctures leave debris on the carriageway. Punctures are one of the major reasons why vehicles stop on the hard shoulder.

Punctures are common, and it is only a matter of time before one happens to you.

Motorists believe that most punctures are caused by sharp objects penetrating the tyre, but that is not the case. Most commonly, they are as a result of weak tyre walls and general deterioration.

Removing shredded tyres from motorway surfaces is a very dangerous job. The golden rule for police officers is never to touch the debris with their bare hands. The debris could be too hot to handle. Exploded tyres are so hot that anyone who touched one would receive severe burns. Sometimes even gloves offer little protection.

The exposed wires are extremely sharp and can cause serious cuts. It is a dangerous combination. That is why police officers do not touch them with their bare hands and you should follow their example.

Let us discuss in more detail what happens if you are driving a car when it suffers a puncture.

As you travel, air in the tyre heats up and expands. If the tyre wall is weak enough, this expansion of air can cause the tyre to explode. As a driver, you will have no warning, no red lights on the dashboard. You will experience an explosion.

What will you experience? If it is a front tyre that has exploded, the steering wheel will spin violently in the direction of the punctured tyre and the steering wheel could be wrenched out of your hands, unless at the time of the puncture, you had both hands on the steering wheel and in a position of being able to exert maximum leverage. The classic 'ten-to-two' or even 'quarter-to-three' position with the hands on the steering wheel would give you the necessary leverage.

If such a hand position were in place, you would be able to control the direction of your vehicle. If you only had one hand on the wheel when the tyre blew, your chances of maintaining control would be blown as well.

A comparison can be made with modern aircraft. All multi-engine aircraft are designed in such a way that if only one engine remains operational, the aircraft can remain flying and land safely. Modern motor vehicles have been designed and engineered to be able to travel in a straight line on three wheels, provided that the driver is holding the steering wheel in the correct position, thus enabling maximum leverage to be exerted.

Who drives with just one hand on the wheel? Drivers who are:

- Using mobile phones.
- Eating.
- Driving with an arm on the door ledge or out of the window.
- Smoking.
- Holding on to the gear lever.
- Retuning the radio.

The more they do it, the more they are putting themselves and others at risk. All of the above, in certain circumstances, can be classed as traffic offences.

Wouldn't it be better to educate drivers of the need to have two hands on the wheel? If what you now know about the consequences of a high-speed blowout was more generally known, there would be fewer people driving one-handed.

Keeping both hands on the steering wheel can save your life.

We will re-emphasise this important point:

Modern technology is such that a car can still be driven in a straight line on three wheels provided the driver has sufficient leverage on the steering wheel.

Knowing what to do if you have a puncture is one thing. How to do your best to avoid one in the first place is another.

Weak tyre walls can be the result of scrubbing your tyres on a footpath, hitting the kerb, incorrect tyre pressures or poor maintenance. The best thing to do is to check your tyres regularly.

Despite your best efforts, if you do suffer a puncture on a motorway, you need to make your way over to the hard shoulder where you can either change the wheel or wait for assistance.

Hard life on the hard shoulder

Most motorway deaths involve slow or stationary vehicles, invariably on the hard shoulder. Consequently, a vehicle parked on the hard shoulder should be regarded as a major hazard.

It may help to understand why. Ask yourself what advice is given to drivers on how to leave the hard shoulder once they have decided to continue their journey. You will not be surprised to learn that the answer is very little.

This motorway patrol vehicle is parked correctly

The cause of the havoc is the fact that drivers know they should only be on the hard shoulder in emergency situations, so when they drive away, they try to rejoin the main carriageway too early. For many drivers, it is a case of first gear, second gear and off we go. This approach can lead to motorway mayhem.

If their vehicle's speed is too slow when they rejoin the motorway, a vehicle travelling behind has to swerve out of the nearside lane to avoid them. The driver in the middle lane has to do likewise. The driver in the outside lane is left with nowhere to go, except the central reservation. The driver in the outside lane is at greater risk than any other driver when a vehicle leaves the hard shoulder.

Beware of any vehicle parked on the hard shoulder. Most drivers have never received any tuition on how to rejoin the main carriageway.

As an aware driver, you do not simply see a vehicle on the hard shoulder, your alert senses are triggered. You are now aware that the driver on the hard shoulder has never been advised how to rejoin the main motorway and will attempt to do so too slowly. You now know the potential knock-on effects.

An aware driver recognises the potential problems and aims to be in space should those problems occur. If the vehicle remains stationary on the hard shoulder you should regard it as a bonus.

If you are on the hard shoulder and want to rejoin the main carriageway what should you do? You should look behind you for a suitable gap in the traffic, build your speed up to match that of the vehicles in the nearside lane, signal your intention, and rejoin the main carriageway when it is safe to do so.

We know this advice sounds simple. *It is.* However, you would be surprised how many drivers are unable to complete this simple task safely.

Surviving the hard shoulder

What do you know about the hard shoulder? What advice do you get about how to behave on it? Sadly, when it comes to basic knowledge about the motorway system and how to use it, the answer is the usual one; very little.

When you park on the hard shoulder, park as close to the grass verge as possible, with your wheels turned to the left. Parking your vehicle at a slight angle to the traffic will make it more noticeable.

Switch your hazard warning lights on and leave them on, even though you risk flattening your battery. Your safety is the most important thing and the warning lights help to ensure that you are seen.

If you are on your own and have a mobile phone, dial 999. Do not telephone a recovery firm or a relative. The police need to know where you are first, in case anything untoward should happen.

If you have suffered a tyre explosion and there is any possibility that you have left debris on the carriageway, *it is your duty* to inform the police as soon as possible. Debris causes further accidents.

If you do not have a mobile phone, locate the nearest emergency telephone, giving your precise position and the details of your problem. How to find the nearest telephone is explained in greater detail later in this section.

Get yourself and your passengers out of the vehicle, onto the grass verge or behind a nearside crash barrier, and as far away from the main carriageway as conditions will allow. Always lock your vehicle if you need to leave it, ensuring there are no valuables visible. Do not allow anyone to wander about on the hard shoulder. Animals should not be allowed out of the vehicle under any circumstances.

After making your call, return to your vehicle and wait for assistance. Keep the vehicle in sight, but stay a safe distance from it. If your vehicle is left unattended for more than 30 minutes, it is likely to be towed away, and the cost of recovery can be very expensive.

Do not, under any circumstances, stand immediately behind or in front of your vehicle. It is very dangerous because when a vehicle approaches you from behind, the driver may not have seen you, or may even have fallen asleep. You could be crushed between the two vehicles.

Never turn your back to oncoming traffic. If this is not possible, keep turning to face the oncoming traffic and check the ever-changing situation. Additionally, listen for the sound of vehicle tyres on the vibra-strip. If you hear a rumbling noise, don't look up, you won't have time. RUN away immediately from the carriageway towards the grass verge.

If you have an offside wheel puncture, get your vehicle as far over to the verge as possible, on it if you can, before you start to change the wheel. If there is someone with you, get them to stand on the verge facing the traffic to warn you of vehicles approaching close to or on the hard shoulder. Listen for the noise of wheels on the vibra-strip.

If you are on your own, consider using the static telephones (ETBs – emergency telephone boxes) to ask if a police patrol vehicle crew could assist you. Any vulnerable person who has to stay in the vehicle should be seated in the front passenger seat with their seatbelt on.

Never leave the motorway to use telephones. The police control room needs to know where you are and will do everything in its power to give you the assistance you require. It will be your link to the 'outside world.'

Telephones on motorways

Static emergency telephones are a common feature on our motorways and are placed not more than one mile apart. On busy stretches and near junctions, there are more.

Should you need to use one of these telephones, locating the nearest one is straightforward.

There are marker posts, normally placed every 100 metres along the edge of the hard shoulder. On the thin edge of the marker post, you will find a silhouette of a telephone and an arrow showing the direction of the nearest one. As the telephones are never more than one mile apart, the nearest one should never be more than half a mile away. These telephones are always placed opposite one another, not offset or staggered, as many motorists believe. The reason they are not offset or staggered is that if a stranded motorist saw a telephone box on the other side of the motorway, they could be tempted to cross six lanes of traffic to reach it. We know that this sounds like a stupid thing to do, but remember, most motorists only act on what they see.

When you lift the handset of one of these emergency telephones, you are connected directly to the operator at the nearest police motorway control room, which is often located at a Police Force HQ. The operator will know exactly where you are as soon as you pick up the telephone, because each one has a unique number. Quoting this number will enable the emergency services to locate your position precisely. This number is so large that it can easily be read whilst travelling in the nearside lane.

There is another way of locating yourself on a motorway. If you are near a junction, tell the operator about the junction sign and quote the number in the bottom left hand corner of the sign. That will locate you in an exact position.

The Centre Lane Owners Club and Members of the Offside Lane Society

When you become an aware driver, you can spot certain tendencies among other motorway drivers. They fall into two categories, and the fundamental characteristic of both is laziness.

The Centre Lane Owners Club (CLOCs). They hog their favourite section of the road regardless of anything or anyone else. 'CLOCs' cause normal traffic flow to become congested because they act as a rolling roadblock, especially when they are slower moving LGVs. They make driving more difficult, because in order to overtake, you have to make lane changes that would otherwise be unnecessary.

Members of the Offside Lane Society (MOLS). They hog the outside lane for mile after mile with no apparent regard for the queue of traffic behind them. They are a close cousin of the 'CLOC.'

There is an argument that states that the laws on overtaking on motorways should be changed, to allow overtaking on the left (known as undertaking). Advocates for change say that if you were able to overtake a slower vehicle on either side, you would have no need to change lanes to pass someone.

What would be wrong with a system like that? All lanes would flow at independent speeds, reducing the necessity to change lanes and constantly lose progress.

In many countries, it is acceptable to overtake on either side of a preceding vehicle. In the UK, it is not, although there are some situations where it is acceptable.

On town centre one-way streets, overtaking on either side is legal and not considered a danger, despite the fact that there are more hazards than on a motorway.

In reality, a motorway is just another one-way street. If it is acceptable in a town centre, then why not on motorways and dual carriageways, where the potential problems are fewer?

The problem is the lack of driver education in relation to overtaking. We are convinced that with a programme of further driver education, the law of overtaking on motorways could be changed. There would be far less congestion, which in turn would enhance the efficiency of the motorway system in general and improve traffic flow.

Those of us who are aware and drive with attitude would have no concerns at being overtaken on either the left or the right.

This legal change could be particularly useful when encountering one of the thousands of 'CLOCs' who congest UK motorways under the present system.

Whilst the law insists that we must overtake only on the right; 'CLOCs' and 'MOLS' are frustrating hazards.

Consider this everyday occurrence. You are driving along a four-lane motorway and there is a 'CLOC' intent on remaining in the third lane out of the four. You are driving quite properly in the nearside lane (lane one out of four). The law presently states that the only lawful way you can pass the 'CLOC' is to cross over to the second lane, then to the third lane and then into the fourth. Having completed your overtaking manoeuvre, you are required to then cross back through the third and second lanes again and into the first.

Other than punctures, one of the most common causes of motorway accidents is changing lanes. Yet we are forced to change lanes by the actions of the 'CLOCs' and 'MOLS.'

What turns otherwise perfectly reasonable drivers into 'CLOCs' or 'MOLS'?

The answer is laziness, ignorance and a lack of consideration for other road users.

When driving along one of the motorway overtaking lanes, less steering effort is required, compared with continually moving to the right to overtake and then moving back to the left after its completion.

What an imposition, to be required to deviate widely from the 'straight-line', (a method advocated because it is safe), simply to get round an unaware and uncaring 'CLOC.'

In this respect it is perhaps understandable why many drivers choose to disregard certain facets of traffic laws and overtake on the left.

There would be no problem with 'CLOCs' and 'MOLS' if you could pass them legally on either side, but not only is overtaking on the left illegal, it is considered highly dangerous, as other drivers do not expect it and are thus not looking for it. Drivers who perform this manoeuvre are not simply risking a fine, but a serious crash too.

The other contribution of 'CLOCs' and 'MOLS' is to increase the annoyance and frustration suffered by other road users. These groups are one of the major causes of an increasing disease suffered by British motorists; 'Road Rage.'

We would never encourage people to break the law, but we do think the law on overtaking on the left needs to be changed in the light of how people actually use our roads.

Whilst on this subject, it is right to point out that there are exceptions to the law. According to the Highway Code Rule 139, overtaking on the left is legal when traffic is moving slowly in a queue, and vehicles in a lane on your right are moving slower than you. The code does not expand on how slowly you have to be going or what constitutes a queue.

Idiots from on high

Increasingly these days there is a new hazard to motorway driving.

In a potentially deadly craze, certain members of society entertain themselves by dropping, throwing, and dangling objects towards the carriageways below. For them it is a game.

Aware drivers should always check out bridges from a distance, though this is not easy during the hours of darkness or poor visibility. If you see someone standing on a bridge directly over a traffic lane, in the ideal world, it's best not to drive directly beneath them. You only have one life so try and keep it.

For the motorway traveller, it is a game that can end in tragedy. If an object any larger than a pebble falls from a bridge and hits a vehicle windscreen, the glass will smash and lives will be put at risk.

Always look out for people on bridges and be particularly vigilant during the evenings, weekends and school holidays.

Other than being aware of the potential danger, there is not a great deal that a driver can do to stop the problem. This is another example of the importance of keeping extended observations and not trusting others. This must become a habit.

If you do see objects being thrown onto a motorway, inform the police as soon as possible.

While on the subject of bridges, there are others on high keeping an eye on you.

Certain motorway bridges have speed cameras attached to them and police patrols sit on these bridges to observe the traffic flow. They are on the lookout for mobile phone users, speeders and so on.

Carriageway markings

There are four different colours of 'cat's eyes' (or reflectors) in use on our motorway carriageways. Red, white, amber and green. They are placed as follows:

- Red to the left, divides the hard shoulder and the first lane.
- Red also divides a merging motorway carriageway running adjacent to the main carriageway, though not at a place where you can join the main carriageway.
- White divides the normal driving lanes.
- Amber divides the outside lane and the central reservation
- Green divides the inside lane from any entrance to, or exist from, the main carriageway.

The idea of coloured 'cat's eyes' is to help drivers pick out the lanes at night or in poor visibility.

Knowing what the different coloured reflectors on a motorway indicate could be vital for you and your VIPs. If you are driving in thick fog and can see in your headlights a row of red 'cats eyes' to the front right of your vehicle, there are two places where you could be. You could be either on the hard shoulder or driving along a merging road running along the main carriageway. Either way, you would need to know.

Motorway service areas

Most drivers do not know which laws govern motorway service areas. When you are driving on a motorway service area, you are on private land and when driving on private land with the owner's permission, you do not need a driving licence, insurance or road-fund licence. However, because a motorway service area is accessible to the general public, the law is applied as if the area was a roadway defined by the Road Traffic Act.

The law regards the perimeter road around the outer edge of the service area as an ordinary road and you are subject to the usual traffic laws when driving on it. It is not a motorway and is not subject to Motorway Regulations.

One striking thing about service areas is the high rate of vehicle crime. It is endemic. Unattended cars parked on a motorway service area are at greater risk of car crime than in town or city centre car parks. Plain-clothes police officers are on duty 24 hours a day on many service areas and they are very busy.

You can reduce the risk to your own vehicle by taking the following precautions:

- Leave your vehicle where it can be seen. In general, try to leave your vehicle in an 'open' space where there are no other vehicles next to it, and not in an isolated corner.

- Do not leave your vehicle alongside high-sided vehicles. Vans, wagons, caravans and buses will obscure the view of your vehicle. The average villain is an opportunist, and if your vehicle is partly hidden it is a more vulnerable target.

- Do not leave anything in sight within the vehicle, even if it is of little value to you. It may not look so to a criminal. Do not leave anything under the seats, especially one of the front seats.

- Your vehicle should be locked and security devices fitted. Always set the alarm, even if you are only leaving the vehicle for a few minutes.

Drivers should be aware that there is a tremendous amount of crime committed on petrol station forecourts, not just on motorway service areas, when vehicles are left unattended. It only takes a second to reach into an unlocked vehicle and steal something. Whenever you go to pay for fuel, lock your vehicle.

Service area entry slip roads

The 'entry' slip road onto many motorway service areas is often shorter than the average slip road and generally has a sharp bend leading into the service area itself.

Drivers are unaware or forget this when they make a service stop. They leave the motorway at high speed and do all their braking in the last few metres.

That leaves a lot of rubber on the road surface and when the road surface is wet, it becomes very slippery.

The perimeter road

The perimeter road can be a normal two-way traffic system. Be careful when travelling along it. Other drivers who have just left the motorway environment do not expect to encounter traffic coming in the opposite direction. They have not had time to assimilate that the Motorway Regulations have ceased and may be travelling faster than they realise and may also be driving on the opposing side of the road.

Exiting the motorway

When it comes to getting off the motorway our advice is simple. Do not be timid.

You should be in control of the situation. If you are driving in one of the overtaking lanes you should return to the nearside lane when you see the half-mile marker sign. When you reach the 300 yard indicator you should consider switching on your left indicator.

Other drivers who are leaving the motorway at the same junction, may not be as well prepared as you. When you have crossed the green cat's eyes and are on the exit slip road, concentrate on the traffic coming off the motorway with you, particularly from your right. Drivers who don't have adequate driving plans leave it until too late and exit the motorway at high speed. Because you are an aware driver, nothing will surprise you.

Finally, it is important to remember that while travelling on the motorway, your tyres will have become very hot, and if one of your brakes has been catching on the disc or drum, that too will have become hot. This will affect your vehicle's ability to brake. For that reason, do not leave your braking until the end of the slip road. Your brakes may not be working as efficiently as when you last used them. Apply your brakes early and gradually and do not be surprised if they cause your vehicle to pull to one side.

The next time you go onto a motorway, your attitude should now be completely transformed. If you regard everyone else as unskilled and unaware and do not expect them to behave properly, you will not be surprised when they do something foolhardy or potentially dangerous.

Motorways: The high-speed challenge

The next section of this book may help to prevent you from picking up a heavy fine, fixed penalty points or a driving ban, and it could help to save your life. It is essential reading.

To an aware driver, travelling too fast and inappropriately through hazardous situations is unacceptable and shows a degree of recklessness towards fellow human beings together with an ignorance of the possible consequences.

With that in mind, let us take a look at the speed limit signs you will see on a motorway.

The new generation of matrix signs could explain the problem ahead and this would have a positive effect on driver compliance. When information is shared, the driver feels respected.

As explained earlier, if you don't require drivers to think, they won't think.

Some matrix signs have red electronic rings around the circumference and are covered by Motorway Traffic Regulations. These signs give orders and MUST be obeyed.

When the authorities take the trouble to display speed limit signs when approaching and driving through road works, they mean it and you can be confident that the limit will be enforced.

White circular speed limit signs, surrounded by a red ring, which display mandatory speed limits, make it easier for the police to prosecute motorists for speeding rather than having to gather evidence to support a case of driving without due care and attention.

Drivers are prosecuted daily for speeding offences through motorway road works. At the time you see them exceeding the speed limit and overtaking you, it may appear that they are getting away without being caught. However, they are being detected.

Electronic matrix signs generally give advice and information. If you ignore the information they give, i.e. '40', and exceed the advised speed limit, this may be used against you in court if you commit a traffic offence.

Despite this legal threat, motorists generally ignore advisory matrix signs. The speed limits displayed are ignored because the reason for the suggested speed limit is not given.

For instance, if you were told to slow down because there was a loose animal or a wheel on the carriageway, the information given could have the desired effect. Most motorists would take notice and slow down. Just to show a number does not provide sufficient information and is not showing the driver any respect.

You should never follow the example of other drivers around you. If you drive at excessive speeds you will be caught. Excessive and inappropriate speed is not something an aware driver considers a virtue. You are an aware driver and a leader, not because you are at the front of a queue, but because you are thinking about your actions and taking responsibility for yourself.

Do NOT become a speeding statistic

Speeding drivers are detected on motorways in the following ways:

Static cameras, used in conjunction with road marking for verification.

Police observation via portable radar.

Unmarked police vehicles equipped with video, radar and on board VASCAR computers, (**V**isual **A**verage **S**peed **C**omputer **A**nd **R**ecorder) which uses fixed points such as white squares painted on the road surface, road markings, a change in the colour of the road surface and shadows caused when vehicles move under bridges.

Pursuit, used as a last option.

You may be surprised to learn that shadows are used to catch speeding drivers. When you are next on a motorway, watch a vehicle in front of you go under a bridge. As the vehicle travels under the bridge, a shadow crosses the back window. That shadow helps to put that vehicle in an exact position. It is as effective as a white square painted on the road surface. These fixed points enable the operator of the police vehicle's on-board computer to place that vehicle in an exact spot and then time that vehicle from there to another chosen point. This enables the police computer to calculate the speed of the vehicle under observation.

Speeding above a posted speed limit is one area where the authorities have found that crime pays. It pays the authorities. The government has discovered that modern methods of speed detection are a great way of raising revenue. If you want to give extra revenue to the government that is your privilege, but be warned, you could soon lose your driving licence.

From a driver awareness point of view, exceeding the posted speed limit is not the real problem.

Speed kills when the wrong people use it in the wrong place.

Inappropriate driving and the lack of proper driver education, are the real problems.

There is great difficulty in defining the word speed.

Motorways: A quiz for the reader

Here are a number of questions related to motorway travel designed to test your knowledge and improve your awareness. Go on, test yourself.

Are three wheeled cars allowed to use a motorway?

Yes.

Are learner drivers lawfully allowed to drive on a motorway?

Yes. Large goods vehicles and passenger carrying vehicles (buses and coaches) are allowed on motorways driven by 'learners.' They already possess 'Full' driving licences and are merely upgrading the classification of their licence.

Drivers who keep good observations on a motorway will notice several tall poles with cameras attached to them. On the top of the pole is a device, which looks similar to a dome or pyramid. They can often be seen on busy stretches of the motorway and around junctions. What are these devices used for?

They are vehicle fume detectors. When traffic flow is affected, either by slow moving or stationary vehicles, there is a build up of exhaust emissions. These devices detect emissions and if these emissions reach high levels, an 'alarm' is triggered in the motorway police control room. The VDUs and monitors in these control rooms are not always manned, and this alarm helps to bring the potential problem to the attention of control room personnel.

Unless there are exceptional circumstances, certain vehicle classifications are not allowed to use the right-hand lane on a motorway, where there are three or more lanes. Can you identify them?

There are three types:

● Goods vehicles with a maximum laden weight over 7.5 tonnes.

● Passenger carrying vehicles (designed to carry more than eight seated passengers in addition to the driver, or over 7.5 tonnes maximum laden weight), buses and coaches.

● Vehicles that pull trailers.

As an aware driver you know that whilst the law might prohibit these vehicles from using the outside lane, this does not mean to say that they won't.

Are the three types of 'prohibited' vehicles allowed to use the third lane on a four-lane motorway?

Yes.

Are the three types of 'prohibited' vehicles lawfully allowed to use the right hand lane on a three-lane motorway if the near side lane is coned off and closed to traffic?

Yes, it is viewed as a special circumstance.

If you possess a 'full' motorcycle licence and wanted to ride a 90c.c. motor cycle on the motorway, would it be lawful to do so?

Yes, but very unwise. It may be lawful, but it is extremely dangerous.

What is the c.c. rating for a motorcycle to become unlawful on a motorway?

Any motorcycle below 50c.c.

On a motorway what is a 'rumble', 'marginal' or 'vibra' strip? Where is it and what is its purpose?

Whatever name it goes by, it is a continual piece of raised white 'tarmac' with ridges, found between the hard shoulder and the nearside lane and on the offside of the motorway carriageway between the right hand lane and the central reservation. Its purpose is to make drivers aware that their vehicle has 'strayed' from the main carriageway.

When following a large maintenance or builder's vehicle along the motorway, an aware driver always expects some debris to fall off the vehicle. However, the potential debris isn't always loaded on the back of the vehicle. Where else (most commonly) could it come from?

The double wheels on the back axle. When maintenance and builders vehicles go 'off-road', these vehicles often pick up stones and house bricks, which can become trapped between the two rear wheels. As the vehicle gathers speed, especially on motorways, these stones and bricks can be thrown backwards at great velocity.

When approaching a queue of stationary traffic on a motorway, how, when and where should you stop?

As an aware driver, you should be travelling with a minimum two-second gap between you and the vehicle in front. You would then see the stationary traffic in good time and be able to stop at least 100 metres away and switch on your hazard warning lights.

You should not move any closer until you are positive that the drivers behind you have seen you and are themselves slowing down. By adopting this defensive stance, you will have time to take evasive action if the following drivers fail to react to your presence. Do not forget to switch off your hazard warning lights when you start to move.

On all roads and especially on motorways, there are many crashes in heavy rain, snow and fog. Why?

The average driver only 'sees' fog, heavy rain and snow, but fog, heavy rain and snow do NOT cause crashes. It is the drivers 'IN' the fog, heavy rain and snow who cause the crashes.

When travelling at 50 mph and above, which device on your vehicle is of no use to you?

The horn. Above 50 mph, the speed at which you are travelling overcomes the horn's ability to transmit its sound forwards. The sound actually goes behind.

The horn presents no problem when used correctly, but nowadays it is used as a form of greeting to other drivers or as a form of rebuke. An aware driver rarely needs to resort to the use of a horn.

Motorway education

You will see that we are strong advocates for improved and increased driver education. That is what inspired us to write **MIND HOW YOU GO**

This is why **MIND HOW YOU GO** publishes general driving and motorway information that in the past only highly trained police drivers received.

By giving you a practical approach to motorway driving, we are taking innovative steps to improve driver education.

The problem about improving driver education goes back to something we covered at the beginning of our journey together. Most drivers think they are experts when they get behind a steering wheel. If you were to ask a cross section of drivers if they felt they had less than average ability when driving on the motorway, how many do you think would admit to it? Whilst there are those who are prepared to admit that they need extra driving education, most would say it is other drivers who need educating. It is a question of egos.

The idea behind this book is to improve general driver awareness.

With the knowledge you have gained from this book, you will realise what is going on around you and what may be going on. This knowledge is a powerful tool. It helps drivers to make better and more informed decisions. It is this knowledge that can save lives.

When you have absorbed the required attitudes and educated yourself on how to think as an aware driver, you will be able to keep your vehicle in as much space as is possible and be able to remain strategically apart from the other drivers.

You can now start to enjoy yourself by observing the best free show on earth without direct involvement.

Situations, which are often portrayed as negative by ordinary drivers, can now become positive to aware drivers.

Remember, when driving along a motorway you are in the same position as the pilot of an aircraft flying in high-speed formation, except you are surrounded by untrained strangers; a very dangerous activity.

The word 'monotony' should not be used to describe motorway driving. (Highway Code, Rule 236). To an aware driver, motorway driving is pure entertainment. Bored drivers are non-planning drivers.

> ### *Stay out of trouble and enjoy yourself.*

Be Ahead of the Game

Security advice for people in the public eye
VIP PROTECTION TECHNIQUES AND ATTITUDES - BASIC POINTS TO CONSIDER.

As an everyday driver, you may not find it necessary to practice all the attitudes and techniques listed below, but if you adopt one or two of them, you will increase your safety. You cannot eliminate risk, but you can reduce it. You only have one life and there is no consolation in being right if you are seriously injured or dead.

Search all vehicles to be used prior to the first journey. Look for signs of interference. (i) Check out any suspicious marks or leaks and check the tyres. (ii) Vehicles are best washed by hand, so you know where all the little, 'acceptable' blemishes are. (iii) Check under the bonnet and in the boot.

All fluid levels must be topped up, especially fuel, as last minute, extended detours may be necessary.

Reconnoitre journeys prior to the visit if possible, so that you are aware of vulnerable and other potential problem areas.

Liase with the VIP as to which side of the vehicle he or she prefers to sit, which will influence nearside or offside pickup and drop-off facilities. If there is no preference, sit the VIP behind the driver, thus providing more physical cover. Remember the 'VIPs wishes.' They are the ones being looked after and paying the bill. They can be advised, but not forced, and will usually accept 'professional' advice.

When approaching the vehicle on foot, always be aware of the oncoming traffic and face it if possible.

After alighting from the vehicle onto the roadway, walk towards the oncoming traffic.

When travelling, keep the doors locked to prevent them being opened from outside. If required, the windows can be opened to a maximum of one inch for fresh air. This will prevent anyone reaching into the vehicle and also prevent objects being thrown into the vehicle.

Try not to come to a complete stop at traffic lights. Look well ahead and keep in mind 'escape routes' at all times.

Always be aware of surroundings and stay alert. Do not relax for an instant. The threat does not diminish until the VIP is in a place of safety.

THE MOST DANGEROUS PARTS OF ANY JOURNEY ARE THE START AND FINISH POINTS, which may be known or anticipated by 'others.'

Keep your route secure. The best security is achieved when the routes are NOT written down, but known only to the drivers.

If journeys are repeated from the same start and finish points, vary your access routes regularly.

When conditions allow, drive at just below 60 mph on dual-carriageways, so that you can be passed without drawing attention to yourself.

A stationary vehicle is potentially more dangerous than a moving one; it may contain a sniper or be a car bomb.

Watch ALL AROUND at all times for pedal cyclists and motorcyclists, especially when travelling in slow moving traffic and town centres. They could attach an explosive device and then disappear. These would usually be on a very short timer, therefore giving little time to respond.

Towards the end of your journey focus more intently. DO NOT become complacent thinking your journey is nearly over. Someone else's actions may just be starting.

Whilst the VIP is in the venue, keep your vehicle nearby and on standby to allow for emergency evacuation.

Give enough time prior to your departure so that the VIP is not kept waiting, which would create a security problem.

Once the VIP is on board, you must move off immediately.

KNOW WHERE ALL 'PLACES OF SAFETY' ARE LOCATED ON THE ROUTE.

Carry a comprehensive first aid kit in the vehicle.

STAY ALERT AND DO NOT RELAX FOR AN INSTANT.

EVERYONE'S SAFETY DEPENDS ON EACH PERSON BEING EVER VIGILANT.

SECTION 5

Additional information on how to reduce the risk of attack - INCLUDING VEHICLE THEFT

Close the windows and lock all the doors when driving in city traffic. If your vehicle comes with automatic locking, make sure it is switched on.

Drive on well-lit, busy roads and avoid shortcuts through unfamiliar or unsafe areas.

Be aware of people who may be following you as you walk to your vehicle.

Avoid parking in a secluded or poorly lit area.

Always have your keys ready to get into the vehicle.

Be aware of 'bump and rob' techniques. You are obliged by law to stop in the event of an accident, but if you are involved in a shunt and are suspicious of the circumstances, remain inside your vehicle with the doors locked and windows shut and call the police. You are entitled to protect yourself under common law and if you think you are in danger, do not stop. Take the registration number of the other vehicle and drive to the nearest police station or police officer, or even a well-lit garage that may have CCTV cameras in operation.

Keep your vehicle keys separate from your house and office keys. Don't leave valuables on show.

Don't put yourself in unnecessary danger and remember that a lot of potential attackers are under the influence of drugs and they do not behave rationally. If someone demands your vehicle keys, don't resist. Hand them over and call the police as soon as possible.

Fitting a tracking device to your vehicle can help it to be located more easily if it has been stolen.

General do's and don'ts

DO

- Check your vehicle for roadworthiness and damage, prior to departure.

- Lock your vehicle if left unattended.

- Check the area behind you before reversing.

- Keep yourself up-to-date with driver legislation.

- Only collect authorised passengers when you drive during your employment.

DON'T

- Leave valuables in view.

- Discuss customer or security information with unauthorised staff.

- Travel with loose pets in your vehicle.

- Drive an unroadworthy vehicle.

- Break the law.

General advice following a breakdown

THE PROCEDURE TO FOLLOW SHOULD YOU BE INVOLVED IN A BREAKDOWN

Take the following action especially if your vehicle breaks down on the motorway.

You should:

Park your vehicle on the hard shoulder with the front wheels turned to the left, and park as far away from the main carriageway as possible, leaving your vehicle parked at a slight angle.

Switch on the hazard warning lights.

Locate the nearest emergency telephone (if appropriate).

Relay your precise position and details of your problem.

Make sure your passengers are out of the vehicle and as far away as possible.

Sit in the front passenger seat with your seat belt on if you have to stay in your vehicle due to disability or illness,.

Always lock your vehicle if you have to leave it.

Return to where you parked your vehicle and await assistance. Keep the vehicle in sight but stay a safe distance from it and the main carriageway.

If you have a puncture, you should:

Stop the vehicle in a safe and lawful place.

Inform the police immediately if there is a possibility of you having left some shredded tyre on the main carriageway.

General advice following a crash

THE PROCEDURE TO FOLLOW SHOULD YOU BE INVOLVED IN A CRASH

You should:

Stop the vehicle and switch off the engine.

Check for any injuries to people involved and beware of fire.

Telephone the Emergency Services (if required).

Check all vehicles and property for damage.

Not admit liability.

Seek witnesses.

Take a photograph or draw a sketch of the accident scene, showing a location marker.

Inform your employer as soon as possible, if applicable.

Exchange insurance details.

Obtain details of any third party (or give them your employer's details).

Give a statement to the police at any reasonable time, not necessarily at the scene but within 24 hours.

Fill in a motor accident claim form as soon as possible, if applicable

If the Form HO/RT/1 has been issued to you, then present it at the police station nearest to where you work. You must obtain the relevant documents from your company and present them to the police within seven days of issue.

SECTION

5

Stay calm and follow the procedures

Driver awareness attitudes – similarities to football and other sporting activity

The reason English FA Premiership football clubs are better than football clubs in other Divisions is that they think about attitudes and techniques a lot more. It's the same when driving a motor vehicle.

The guiding principles and philosophies of Driver Awareness Limited have been fully incorporated into this book and experience shows that they work.

Football managers instil their players with the benefits of belief, discipline, self-assurance and composure. These attributes ensure that players play the game in space and think ahead. When driving on the road with these qualities in mind, you will enjoy a much safer driving experience.

Everything in this book guides you towards thinking about your actions. By taking responsibility for yourself, and keeping things simple, you will stay out of trouble.

There are several parallels that can be drawn between good drivers and good sportsmen and women.

The following points illustrate these parallel qualities.

MIND HOW YOU GO

Belief – That you are more aware than other road users and that education and knowledge, when used in the right way, keep you ahead of the game.

Discipline – Other road users are untrained and are not to be trusted. Aware drivers never take example from them.

Self-Assurance – Don't break the rules. Take responsibility for yourself.

Composure – Aware drivers make it look easy. To show surprise towards other road users, no matter what they try to do to you, is to trust them. Aware drivers NEVER trust anybody.

Aware Drivers - should regard other road users as untrained. Through no fault of their own, they are not up to your standard.

When other road users are behaving themselves, it's only a bonus.

Aware Drivers - command the road. A slow, timid and negative driver will be abused.

Be the leader and be deliberate, though without aggression.

Aware Drivers – by driving in as much available space as possible you give yourself time to think, 'What am I going to do about this?' Give yourself space in which to escape.   Do not drive only on what you see. By looking a long way ahead and seeing the whole picture with a 'what if?' factor, you will have time to consider the circumstances reasonably expected to develop.

Aware Drivers – are leaders on the road.

> ***Safe and aware drivers are thinkers and not just good at physical driving skills.***

Summary of an Aware Driver

Summary of an Aware Driver

At the beginning of this book we explained that the aim was to persuade you to change your mind-set whenever you sit behind a steering wheel.

Part of this process means regarding other drivers as potential dangers.

We would never suggest that you go through life thinking lowly of your fellow human beings. The opposite is the case. We have respect for our fellow human beings and feel compelled to try and help to stop the carnage on our roads.

You should now be aware that, as a road user, your life is at risk. That should be the starting point for any journey.

The advice outlined along the way provides you with a practical way to reduce risks. We hope you will now put these techniques into practice. You should now be more aware of actual and potential dangers on our roads.

When a mistake is made, you will recognise it and become less inclined to blame something or someone else.

Whilst you are entitled to pass comment and have opinions about other drivers, you should never be surprised by their actions. If you find yourself complaining, it is YOU who has the attitude problem.

To supplement the skills you picked up as a learner driver, you are now equipped with the knowledge about how a driver should think, and you have no excuse for losing your composure.

If you have the desire to increase your awareness when you are driving, you will need to gain knowledge. Once you have started to gain knowledge, your skill will increase, and having increased your skill, you will find you will want to gain further knowledge. It's a full circle, and your habits will become self-generating.

It is up to you to adopt these habits and 'new' driving style and when you do, you will discover that your driving will become a pleasurable experience, both for you and your passengers, and they will tell you. It is extremely reassuring and comforting to be carried in a vehicle when the driver is relaxed, confident and in control.

In contrast, try to remember what it felt like when you were last a passenger with someone who was constantly ranting and raving at other drivers. How safe did you feel? How quickly do you want to repeat that experience?

There would be no need for this book if overall driving standards in this country were good. Unfortunately they are not. When you have mastered the lessons contained here, you are not going to change the world on your own. However, you will be able to take responsibility for your own actions.

When you suspect other drivers are trying to do you a mischief, turn this negative situation into a positive one. It is all about anticipation, the making of a plan, linked to time and space, which will enable you to keep your vehicle safe and away from the destructive tendencies of others. Use the power you have gained from wisdom as a force for good.

You can remain a good example to other road users, reduce your stress levels and stay safe, healthy and alive.

Happy motoring and remember:

When other road users are behaving themselves, it's only a bonus.

You are now an aware driver.

Always think ahead, stay in space

and

MIND HOW YOU GO

You are now an aware driver and when you next find yourself in a queue of traffic, remember who the leader really is. You may eventually drive away and follow the traffic, but you do so as a leader, taking responsibility for yourself.

Pause for Thought

This next section of the book is designed to exercise the mind and all that's asked is,

'What do *you* think?'

'What do *you* Think?'

If you think education is expensive, try ignorance

In 1934, Leslie Hore-Belisha became the Minister of Transport in Great Britain. Before he became Minister of Transport, motorists were allowed to drive without having to pass a driving test; anyone could apply for a driving licence and proceed to drive, which resulted in carnage on the roads

Hore-Belisha could see the need to have a system whereby motorists had to reach a certain level of competence in order to improve safety on the road. He introduced driving tests for all motorists, oversaw a substantial revision of the Highway Code, which had first been published in 1931, and introduced pedestrian crossings, which greatly reduced the number of accidents involving pedestrians. These crossings were illuminated by large orange lights on the top of black and white poles, and quickly became known as 'Belisha Beacons', the forerunner of the pelican crossings we are all familiar with today.

He also realised that in order to enforce our road traffic laws correctly, the police needed to be better drivers than the general public and to this end, he established Police Driving Schools throughout the country. Very soon, British Police 'Class One' Drivers were the most highly trained drivers in the world and 'British Police Trained' was a description that immediately commanded great respect.

Over the next fifty years, the police gained a vast amount of knowledge through dealing with every conceivable road and traffic situation that motorists would ever encounter. Police forces from all over the world came to the UK to learn from our experience and expertise.

However in 1989, following the advent of 'political correctness', it was decided that these high standards were 'elitist.' The 'Class One' category was replaced with 'Police Advanced' and standards began to decline. In the old 'Class One' days it was common for approximately 50% of the trainees to fail a police driving course. Now, in some areas, everyone passes. Standards are much lower, and it shows.

These days, it is not uncommon to see police officers driving police vehicles while not wearing a seat belt, or with only one hand on the steering wheel in order to smoke, use a mobile phone or personal radio. You might see them parking their vehicle on the footpath or within the zigzag lines on the approach to a pedestrian crossing; all situations which, in earlier days, would have resulted in the officer involved being subjected to disciplinary action and having their driving permit suspended.

The sooner the police get back to the old standards and forms of discipline, the better. There is a lot of experience waiting to be utilised by way of former officers who are only too willing to assist. In years to come, all this experience will no longer be available and it will be a sad loss, never to be replaced.

The modern police force is funded by the government and county councils. Certain aspects of road safety have become politicised, and today's Chief Constables have largely become subservient to politicians who do not have the knowledge and experience of the police themselves. As a result of this and because of the way road safety matters are now funded, the Chief Constables are somewhat reluctant to stamp their authority for fear of political reprisal.

Should a Chief Constable dare to speak up about the inadequacies of the decisions of government and county councils, the likelihood is that this action will be seen as that of a 'maverick.'

The police force should be in a position to work 'with' councils and not 'for' them in order to improve matters.

In view of this, we will now illustrate some of the inconsistencies and irregularities that contribute towards the mess into which this country has plunged in relation to some road safety matters.

As an aware driver you realise that things are not always what they seem.

The following pictures are published to enable you to see what our authorities have allowed to happen and to enable you to form your own opinions regarding their correctness. The captions beneath the photographs expose the thoughtlessness of their ideas.

'What do *you* think?'

Ambiguous road signs

The Highway Code states that signs with **Red Circles** are mostly prohibitive, (i.e. 'You Must Not Do'). Plates below signs qualify their message.

Signs with **Blue Circles**, but no red border, mostly give positive instruction, (i.e. 'You Must Do').

This mini-roundabout has a circular sign with a blue background.

This is a photograph of an ordinary saloon car, clearly illustrating that it is unrealistic and impractical for this vehicle to travel completely around this mini-roundabout without straddling it, yet the Highway Code states that all vehicles MUST pass round the central markings, the exception being large vehicles which are physically incapable of doing so. Nowhere does it define what 'large' means, neither does this sign display a plate that qualifies the message about large vehicles.

There are many different sizes of vehicle on our roads, some much larger than others, yet the blue sign actually states that YOU MUST go around this mini-roundabout and 'give-way' to vehicles approaching from the immediate right.

This mini-roundabout and sign are typical of thousands of others constructed throughout this country which are similar both in design and positioning.

This is an official road policy which not only brings the law into disrepute, but also leads to discrimination between one vehicle driver and another.

It is the opinion of the authors of this book that these 'blue-background' circular signs should be replaced with 'give-way' signs similar to the 'four-way' junction signs used in the USA. They work equally well at junctions and do not bring the law into disrepute by discriminating between drivers.

On most motorway service areas, the perimeter road is designated 'a road' under the Road Traffic Act, and is under the authority of the Highways Agency, the County Council and the police.

The following four photographs, taken on motorway service areas, show signs which are ill-informed and bring the law into disrepute.

This sign, placed at the end of a motorway slip road at the entrance to a motorway service area, whilst still located on a designated 'road', actually states 'You must not drive slowly.' How irresponsible can a sign like this be?

This is a purpose-made lay-by for 'long loads.' This sign actually states 'long loads are not allowed.'

Here is a pedestrian crossing situated on 'a road.' This sign has a red circle. What does this sign actually say? 'Pedestrians are not allowed.'

These signs are situated at the exit of a service area parking area at it's junction with the service area perimeter road. (i.e. a designated 'road' under the Road Traffic Act). These signs actually state, 'You must NOT give-way or drive in either direction!'

The following photographs are taken on ordinary roads and show traffic signs which require some thought.

This is a correct 'give way' sign. It is a triangular sign which gives the driver an 'order.'

What is the difference between this triangular sign which gives an 'order', and other triangular signs which give 'warnings?' Answer: This is a triangular sign which is inverted.

No left turn – NOT allowed

No right turn – NOT allowed

No U turns – NOT allowed

Try and workout the meaning of this sign. This sign is a triple negative. No U turns – are not allowed (the order has been crossed out) and then it 'ends.'

Please note that the previous 'no right', 'no left' and 'no U turn' signs whilst incorrect, are still considered 'lawful' and 'must be obeyed.'

We consider from the captions beneath the photographs, the 'no right', 'no left' and 'no U turn' signs, as depicted, are 'double negatives.' The sign tells you NOT to do something and then the red coloured bar cancels that instruction.

As Great Britain is now within the European Community, consistency of road signage is imperative. Those readers who are familiar with the road signs on the continent will know that on the approach to a village, a round sign with a red circle and a figure displayed, will state the posted speed limit that must not be exceeded whilst driving through the village. On leaving the village, there will be another round sign with a red circle which displays the same speed limit but this sign will have a diagonal red coloured bar through it; this means 'end of speed limit.'

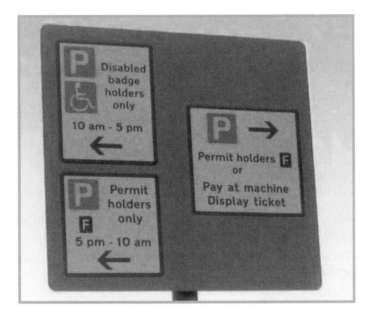

At first glance, for vehicles parking to the left of this sign, the words indicate a parking area for 'Disabled badge holders only 10am – 5pm.' But does it?

When you have knowledge, it can also read, 'Disabled badge holders are only allowed between 10am and 5pm.'

The same logic applies to 'Permit Holders.'

Ambiguous signs like this should not be used by councils to enforce parking regulations.

The signs in the following photographs state the obvious to a thinking driver. We believe they are often surplus to requirements.

The next time you are a passenger in a vehicle, ask the driver, having just driven past a warning sign, what that sign said. Generally speaking the driver will not be able to tell you.

When you are driving along a country lane do you need to be told by a sign that there is a possibility of sheep or cows in the road?

Do you need to be warned, by a sign, that there's a possibility of tractors using the road?

At this stage in the book, it should be clear to you that:

> # Good aware drivers do not need warning signs; bad drivers never use them.

According to these signs, A) here is a village without children and B) here is a street without elderly people.

This is a warning sign that is useful and has a purpose. 'Drivers of high vehicles should consider finding another route.'

Examples of council folly

This deviation marking on the nearside of a major road is both unnecessary and useless. What possible purpose can this red paint have on a perfectly straight road?

Drivers under police instruction are told to drive in as much available space as possible. This practice is known as the 'Safety Position.'

If being 'in space' is the safest position to be on a road, why has this council (like many other councils) been allowed to reduce the usable width of this road by building chicanes and footpath build-outs with black metal posts. The example above is on a very busy bus route. Traffic calming measures like this show how the authorities will do anything except address the problem of 'the driver', the majority of whom already have problems by colliding with hazards!

Is this common sense? Why do authorities paint bus stops in the middle of the road, alongside footpath build-outs, and opposite one another? This is a photograph taken on a major 'A' Class road.

Look at these two photographs. The worst place to overtake a cyclist is opposite the bollard in the middle of the road.

Why has this council been allowed to construct a ten metre long cycle lane in the worst place for a cyclist to be overtaken? This is not an isolated occurrence. This practice of thoughtlessness when marking out our roads is replicated throughout the country. Police driver training policy is for cyclists to be allowed a minimum side-on wobble distance of at least six feet (two metres) when being overtaken, and if such a gap is not possible, the cyclist should not be overtaken.

There are many reasons why cyclists 'wobble.' They wobble to avoid debris or standing water in the roadway, a vehicle door may open, a gusty wind may blow them off course or most commonly, when the cyclist stands on the pedals to pedal up a hill. Whatever the reason, cyclists will always 'wobble.'

As previously stated, the majority of drivers drive mainly on what they see and when they see a cycle lane which is just three feet wide, (as shown before) they will often drive too close to that painted cycle lane. The cyclist is then in greater danger than if there was no cycle lane at all.

With all of this in mind, why are councils allowed to paint cycle lanes that are less than six feet wide?

Consider this. The above cyclist is in less danger than if he was in the cycle lane shown in the previous photograph. Good aware drivers do not need white paint to make themselves and other road users safe.

'Lancashire Cycleway.' What cycleway? One without a designated cycle lane!

These signs are endemic throughout the country and we believe, as aware drivers, that if you need to be told there may be cyclists on any road, then you should not be driving in the first place.

These signs are a complete waste of taxpayers' money.

Later in this book we elaborate on the effect of road markings and their contribution towards congestion and pollution.

If you went to the coast and stood on the edge of a cliff, you would not expect to see a sign which stated, 'Sky' 'Sea' 'Horizon.' That would be ludicrous.

Yet, in the main, the signs shown in these examples are just as ludicrous.

Having now seen these photographs, and the ambiguity they display, it is clear that the authorities have given little thought, or don't know what they are doing, when it comes to leading by example.

We have exposed hypocrisy and inconsistency in this book, and maintain that the best way to improve matters is by proper driver education.

This education should be based on the previous high standards that the police maintained before government 'spin' took over. This previous knowledge, discipline and common sense would achieve better results than the 'knee-jerk' policies currently adopted in an effort to solve the very serious problem of saving lives and preventing injuries on our roads.

Did you know?

This may seem an obvious question. Why do you have to stop at a red traffic light?

It is a lawful sign and must be obeyed. The red light is circular; it gives an order.

Originally a red traffic light had the word 'Stop' written on the lens, but this is no longer the case.

Now take this logic a step further.

Green traffic lights are also mostly circular and, as stated above, circular signs give orders.

However, the Highway Code states 'A green light means you may go on if the way is clear. Take special care if you intend to turn left or right and give way to pedestrians who are crossing.'

Originally a green traffic light had the word 'Go' written on the lens, but this is no longer the case.

Circular signs give orders, but in our view, there should never be an order to tell a driver to 'go.' We believe that all green traffic lights should be illuminated with directional arrows that don't give orders, but merely state 'you may go on if the way is clear.'

These yellow lines over the edge of the footpath indicate loading and unloading restrictions on roads other than Red Routes. The number of lines used indicate various operational time restrictions. What is not generally known, is that loading and unloading also INCLUDES the setting down and the picking up of your passengers.

A flashing indicator doesn't mean anything to an aware driver. This vehicle is only turning left when it does so. Do not assume it is turning left simply because the indicator is flashing.

Double White Lines in the centre of the road

Double white lines in the middle of the road are enforceable by law only when they have reflective studs integrated into their markings. It is an offence to park your vehicle alongside these lines. Some drivers are unaware that it is an offence to park alongside these lines, whether they are broken or solid. The vehicles shown above appear to be parked illegally. The drivers of these vehicles risk a fine and licence endorsement.

The white line painted in the gutter does not mean 'clearway.' It has no meaning in law. It marks out the edge of the carriageway. It is just white paint. The double white lines in this picture do not have reflective studs integrated into their markings and therefore do not comply with the regulations regarding enforcement laws.

If you are sure there are no other road users on a road like the one shown above, there is no need to slavishly follow this white paint. You can drive in as straight a line as possible, but remember to keep in mind the 'what if?' factor.

On single-carriageway roads, in order to outline the perimeter of a curve, lampposts are generally erected on the perimeter edge only. This policy is particularly useful when there is poor visibility.

Farmers are responsible for their walls, hedges and fences. However, these railings have been erected by a council and are known as 'Open' or 'Easy View Railings', for obvious reasons; they give road users a much better view into what would otherwise be a zone of invisibility.

By spending money in this way, this council has greatly improved matters in relation to road safety rather than, as we have previously outlined in this book, generally acted against the interest of the road user.

Quiz Answers

How does the aware driver think when...?

These are the answers to the questions on page 37.

Ask yourself what you would do as an aware driver in these everyday scenarios.

1 *A traffic light is showing 'green' in your favour?*

The Highway Code states, 'A green light means you may go on if the way is clear.'

However, most drivers would say 'green means go' and as you can see, that statement is incomplete. It actually means you may proceed if it is safe to do so and you can clear the junction.

In your mind's eye, think of all traffic light junctions as having yellow boxes painted on the road surface. Do not enter the junction unless it is safe to do so and your exit is clear.

2 *A traffic light is showing 'red' against you?*

You must 'stop.'

However, a red light does not mean there is a physical barrier to stop other traffic. Many motorists and cyclists travel through red lights.

When it comes to traffic light junctions, there is no consolation being involved in a collision with a motorist who has driven through a red light, and then saying, 'It was your fault.'

Many motorists are lying in our hospitals seriously injured because it was not their fault. It is better not to be there in the first place.

Timidity is not the answer when driving through a junction. It takes a minimal effort by drivers to glance into side junctions on their approach and to take evasive action if necessary, which could save their lives.

SECTION **8**

3 *You are approaching a zone of invisibility?*

An aware driver does not trust anyone or anything.

Most crashes happen because drivers do not consider the possibility of a serious hazard being hidden in a zone of invisibility. Other road users generally react to what they can see, whereas an aware driver also considers the 'what if?' factor.

Hazards which are not readily visible to others are a liability. As far as aware drivers are concerned, all other road users, be they around a corner or a bend, hiding behind a stationary obstruction or even more deadly, travelling behind an oncoming vehicle, will pull out with no proper view for themselves. They do not have driving plans and take no account of the actual and potential danger.

When met by one of these potential killers, it is no consolation to be right and dead. Maintaining your own space and keeping yourself out of trouble is vital.

To liken this to VIP protection duties and to put this scenario into a security situation; a criminal will usually commit a deed in a place where it is difficult to be seen.

4 *You are following a moving bus?*

This bus is going to stop at the next bus stop. If it does not stop, it's only a bonus.

Most drivers only drive on the basis of what they see. They see the moving bus.

There is no thought in the driver's head as to what that bus is about to do. It is only when the bus begins to slow down that the following driver starts to think about the situation that may develop. If the bus stops, the likelihood is that the driver will become trapped behind the stationary bus, thus reducing visibility and making it difficult to proceed with safety.

As an aware driver, you know that the bus may stop. You have considered the 'what if?' factor. If the bus stops, it will become less of a problem to you and you can proceed to overtake in as straight a line as possible.

5 *You are approaching a stationary bus?*

This bus is going to move off.

You need to be aware that there will be people around, either having alighted from the bus or running to catch it. If the bus doesn't move off and there is no one around, it's only a bonus.

6 *You are approaching a right-hand bend?*

As you approach a right-hand bend, you should position your vehicle towards the left hand side of the carriageway.

The basic thought when approaching a right hand bend should be, 'Where is the correct position for me to gain the best advantage to negotiate this bend safely?'

For every inch that you move your vehicle towards the nearside of the carriageway, you will increase your sight line and greatly enhance the view around the bend. This position also places you furthest away from any approaching vehicle.

You will then negotiate the bend with the least centrifugal force acting upon your vehicle (the force that pushes a vehicle towards the left on a right-hand bend), and you will be in as straight a line as possible, thus increasing stability.

This positioning advice does not mean that you should allow your wheels to be on the debris in the gutter, or to let your vehicle 'skim' nearside junctions or parked vehicles.

In the above photograph, the white line painted on the left is forcing motorists, who only drive on the basis of what they see, into a very unwise road position. A driver negotiating a right hand bend should never feel comfortable driving towards the middle of the road.

7 *You are approaching a left-hand bend?*

As you approach a left-hand bend, you should position your vehicle towards the centre of the road.

The basic thought when approaching a left hand bend should be, 'Where is the correct position for me to gain the best advantage to negotiate this bend safely?'

For every inch that you move your vehicle towards the centre of the road, you will increase your sight line and greatly enhance the view around the bend.

You will then negotiate the bend with the least centrifugal force acting upon your vehicle (the force that pushes a vehicle towards the right on a left-hand bend), and you will be in as straight a line as possible, thus increasing stability.

This positioning advice does not mean that you should allow your vehicle, either actually or potentially, to travel too close to oncoming vehicles.

8 *You are approaching a left-hand bend but a vehicle is parked on your offside just prior the bend?*

You should always consider the circumstances that may reasonably be expected to develop.

The parked vehicles shown in the above picture will be seen by an oncoming driver who will then have to negotiate them by positioning their vehicle towards the middle of the road.

The aware driver anticipates this situation and will not be in the middle of the road on the approach to this left-hand bend.

9 *You are approaching parked vehicles on your near side?*

Leave a gap between your vehicle and a parked vehicle, of at least four feet (the width of a door).

If you cannot pass leaving this amount of space, you should reduce your speed and be ready to stop.

One of the parked vehicles may move out, a door may open, or someone may walk between the vehicles into the roadway.

10 *You are approaching parked vehicles on your near side but some of them may be on the 'wrong side' of the road, facing you?*

When you see a vehicle parked on the 'wrong side' of the road, you must be aware that if that vehicle leaves its parking space, its driver cannot see the oncoming traffic.

The utmost care should be taken when passing these vehicles because the driver cannot see the oncoming traffic until he moves out. Passengers of parked vehicles also pose a danger because they will often open their doors into the carriageway without looking or thinking about the consequences.

11 *You are approaching a pedal cyclist?*

A pedal cyclist must be given a side-on wobble distance of at least six feet.

There are many reasons why cyclists 'wobble.' They wobble to avoid debris or standing water in the roadway, a vehicle door may open, a gusty wind may blow them off course or most commonly, when the cyclist stands on the pedals to pedal up a hill. Whatever the reason, cyclists will always 'wobble.'

An aware driver does not need white paint on the road outlining a cycle track to know that you should give a cyclist a side-on gap of at least six feet.

If a cyclist cannot be given a minimum six foot 'wobble' distance, they should not be overtaken.

12 *You are driving along a country lane?*

You should expect to find people, tractors and farm animals in the roadway.

An aware driver does not need a warning sign indicating the possibility of cattle, sheep or a tractor when driving through the countryside.

Don't be surprised when you see a cyclist, people walking in the roadway, or a large vehicle around the next bend.

SECTION **8**

13 *You are driving when it starts to rain for the first time in two weeks?*

The road surface is likely to be extremely slippery.

Here is a little science lesson. When vehicles travel along the road they leave deposits of rubber from their tyres on the road surface. Tyre rubber is an oil-based product. When it rains, the rain water sits on this film of oil and produces a slippery surface. Diesel oil produces the same effect.

The most dangerous areas tend to be where vehicles brake and accelerate around corners and on the approach to roundabouts.

The worst example of a slippery road surface in the rain is the exit slip road from a motorway leading into a service area. These roads are generally short and when vehicles leave the main carriageway at high speeds, they brake harder and leave large amounts of rubber on the road surface.

The same principle was put to use when road safety organisations created skidpans, which gave drivers the opportunity to experience a skid and gain confidence in controlled surroundings. A small amount of oil was laid down on a private tarmac surface and then sprayed with copious amounts of water.

An aware driver does not need a sign warning of a 'slippery road' the next time it rains following a dry spell.

14 *You are waiting in a side road in order to join a main road. A vehicle coming from your right, on the main road, has its left-turn indicator flashing?*

Do not believe this signal.

This vehicle may be turning into your junction, it may be stopping either before or after your junction, it may be signalling having just overtaken another vehicle, or the driver may have forgotten to cancel the signal. A flashing indicator just confirms that the bulb works.

With this in mind, timidity can be a major problem when driving a motor vehicle. If the vehicle on the main road is sufficiently far away, there is no need to remain in the junction. If there are no other vehicles around, (especially motor cyclists) and it is safe to do so, then by all means, make your move.

Authorities in Need of Education

Authorities in need of education

With the current proliferation of speed cameras and the reduction of traffic patrols on our roads, some motorists are getting away with reckless and dangerous driving, which manifests itself in bad manners and inappropriate road behaviour.

It is clear that those in authority, such as council officials, senior policy decision making police officers and members of our so-called road safety groups do not recognise, or choose to ignore, the human element.

As this book demonstrates, there is a *new way*; a very effective and successful way to approach road safety matters.

Should the government eventually address the true cause of road accidents (crashes) by introducing a well informed, effective driver education programme to deal with the problems caused by inattentive driving, aggressive attitudes and the real dangers of decision making based on 'assuming' how other road users will behave, you will know that it is serious about reducing death and serious injury on our roads.

Once this education programme is in place, the authorities can then follow up with a firm law and order policy because people will know what they are doing and will not be in a position to complain. It will be a matter of 'It's not what you do; it's knowing what to do.'

Improvements in road safety cannot happen overnight, but if the government (which is ultimately responsible for safety on our roads) was to base its programme on the techniques outlined in this book, our roads would become much safer and the number of crashes would decrease dramatically.

The objective of this book is not primarily to confront authority, but to highlight the dreadful mess this country has descended into as a result of many of the current road safety practices.

> ## Building hazards in front of drivers who are already colliding with hazards is a nonsense.

Who can now doubt that there is an urgent need for change, and a fresh direction? If the authorities do not recognise the need for <u>proper</u> driver education, it is they who are in need of education.

What does the future hold?

Congestion, road pollution and crashes are blighting modern society, yet there are a number of simple remedies that can overcome some of these problems.

Here are some suggestions:

Firstly; there are large cumbersome buses.

Large buses are a primary cause of diesel fume pollution. They cause obstruction and unnecessary congestion which costs millions of pounds in lost productivity. Most buses, at off-peak times, are near empty. Why do buses have to be so big?

Secondly; many traffic lights could be switched off during 'off-peak' hours.

A 'four-way' flashing amber light in this instance would mean; 'give-way' and proceed only if it is safe to do so.

When traffic lights are not working, drivers slow down; they look into the opposing junctions for oncoming traffic and take extra care before proceeding. At 'off-peak' times, the likelihood is there would not be a queue on the approach to the junction. Drivers are capable of sorting themselves out without causing a problem.

When the traffic lights are in operation and the signal shows a 'green' light, what do drivers do? They drive straight through the junction with no regard for the potential hazard of a driver, or a cyclist, who may not have seen, or chosen to ignore, the 'red' traffic light in the opposing junction.

The lesson to be learned here is: If you don't require drivers to think, they won't think.

Whilst on the subject of traffic lights, we are supporters of the American system of filtering at a junction, into the flow of traffic, when a 'red' traffic light signal is being displayed. The system requires drivers to look and think about their actions, and certainly helps to improve the flow of traffic, thus reducing congestion and pollution.

Thirdly; A government regulation states that certain LGV and PCVs (large goods vehicles and passenger carrying vehicles) must be fitted with speed limiters.

We are firm believers that you should not take away the control of a vehicle from the driver.

In the picture above, there is nothing unlawful taking place with this wagon occupying the right hand lane on a two lane motorway. However, by fitting a speed limiter, or governor as they are known, the opportunity for the vehicle in the outer lane to increase its speed and overtake the vehicle in the nearside lane as quickly as possible is removed. This causes a situation where the 'overtaking' vehicle can be alongside the 'slower' vehicle for mile after mile, a situation you may have witnessed. On a busy motorway, this will cause congestion and could lead to frustration in the drivers held up in the resulting tail-back of traffic.

An additional problem with speed limiters is driver fatigue. When driving a vehicle at a constant speed, a monotonous engine noise is created in the cab. When coupled with the night-time driving environment many goods vehicle drivers work in, this can cause severe drowsiness. It is not surprising to know that some of these drivers fall asleep at the wheel.

Take away the thinking requirement from drivers and the situation becomes worse. There are no exceptions.

Could you live with this control?

With the technology currently available, it is possible to incorporate a 'chip' into the electronics of the engine of every vehicle which could be accessed by a satellite system and then be used to govern the speed of that vehicle to keep it within the posted limit. In other words, external technology could be used to control your car. Such a system is currently being reviewed by our government, the practicalities of which are seriously flawed.

A similar system has already been tried and found wanting.

In the early 1970s, the government, when authorising the building of our motorway network, had incorporated into the construction of the carriageways a series of electronic sensors which were capable of detecting the number of vehicles which travelled along the road, together with the speed at which these vehicles were travelling.

This system, 'Motorway Inductive Detection and Signalling' (MIDAS), was intended to be used by the government to control the speed and flow of traffic on the motorway.

The government proposal was to make it compulsory for each vehicle manufacturer to build into every new vehicle, an engine management system which could be detected by MIDAS, so that when a vehicle was travelling too fast or too close to another vehicle, i.e., 'slipstreaming', the control technology would be activated and reduce the engine speed to slow down that vehicle.

The government conducted controlled experiments with this system, but quickly realised its short-comings. The MIDAS system still lies beneath some motorway carriageways, though it is now used solely for detecting congestion of traffic flow, and can automatically activate the matrix signs.

We believe that driver education is the best way forward to improving road safety, and whilst satellite technology has many benefits, taking away control of the vehicle from the driver is not one of them. The idea may seem admirable, but would create more problems than it cured. For such a system to work, every vehicle would have to have this technology fitted simultaneously and that is not possible.

The ramifications of introducing a system of control, when not all vehicles could respond to it, are enormous.

Consider the situation that would arise if you were travelling along a motorway in driving rain which creates excessive road spray, and you needed to accelerate in order to remain safe, when suddenly, your engine were to cut out because satellite technology had over-ridden your engine speed without recognising your need to increase your speed. If the vehicle immediately behind you was not fitted with this 'automatic cut-off' system, you would be in trouble and there would be a great possibility of a serious crash. If a serious injury, or worse still, fatality occurred as a result of the government stopping your engine, who would be liable? This scheme would be a lawyer's dream.

Furthermore, who would consider buying a vehicle fitted with a device which gave the authorities control to stop your engine, thus putting your life at risk?

One series of controls we do agree with is the need to have regular tests for eye-sight, driver reaction times, hazard perception and body/eye co-ordination. This should be incorporated within a more rigorous driving test. Hazard perception tests, as they stand today, are regarded by many driving instructors as an inadequate exercise and a joke.

A further improvement in road safety could be made by the government introducing legislation whereby all insurance companies would be directed to reduce insurance premiums year on year for those drivers who had remained clear of a blameworthy crash and maintained an endorsement free licence.

In conclusion

Aware drivers should never be surprised at the actions or inaction of other drivers.

Driving should be enjoyable and how you THINK can make it so.

In the future, should you find yourself making exclamations of surprise at the actions or inaction listed below, you will now realise where the problem lies; **YOU** will have been trusting the other driver.

Aware drivers always expect other drivers to:

- Lack any proper driver education.

- Abuse you whilst you drive.

- Drive within a few feet of your rear bumper.

- Leave the motorway hard shoulder at a slow speed.

- Overtake on the left.

- Pull out of junctions directly in front of you.

- Show no courtesy.

- Drive slowly along narrow country roads with no regard for a following vehicle.

- Have poor eyesight.

- Have slow reaction times.

Aware drivers always expect other drivers to be unaware and naively say:

- 'Speed Kills.'

- 'The road is dangerous.'

- 'The weather caused an accident.'

- 'Driving on a motorway is boring.'

- 'I assumed.'

- 'I presumed.'

- 'Keep your distance.'

- 'Traffic calming measures are a good idea.'

- 'Slow drivers are always careful.'

- 'Driver education is not the answer towards improving road safety.'

Aware drivers know what to do in relation to the above.
They turn negative situations around by adopting a positive attitude.

Aware drivers do not break the law. They are leaders
and do not take example from others who only think they are experts.

Years of previous driving habit cannot be changed overnight, but driver awareness attitudes and techniques can help you to form new habits which will become a way of life from now on.

There are millions of bad drivers on our roads whom you cannot do anything about. By adopting this new way of driver thinking, you can let the world pass you by. No single individual will change the world, but without putting yourself on a pedestal, you can gain awareness, learn to live with it and survive. It doesn't matter who is in the right or wrong. Just make sure others don't get you.

The authors of this book recognise the problems on our roads and offer a *new way* to achieve a more acceptable means of delivering proper driver education, which in turn will help to keep our roads a safer place in which to be.

In accordance with the attitudes of British Police VIP protection driving techniques, the criteria for all drivers on every day roads should be:

- You must have a complete non-trusting attitude towards other road users.

- You should always drive in as much available s p a c e as possible.

- You should look as far ahead as possible and do not drive just on the basis on what you see. Always consider the 'what if?' factor.

Take responsibility for yourself

You can be a good example to other road users,
reduce your stress levels and stay safe, healthy and alive.

Happy motoring and remember:

When other road users are behaving themselves, it's only a bonus.

You are now an aware driver.

Always think ahead, stay in space

and

MIND HOW YOU GO

If you have any suggestions or wish to contact the authors, please visit our website.
www.mindhowyougo.co.uk

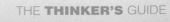

Index

A

About the Authors
    Adrian Shurmer   4.
    Steve O'Donnell   5.
Abuse of the Vehicle   13.
Acceleration Sense   33. 59. 68. 74.
Accidents   16-18. 20. 162.
Acknowledgements   2.
Ambiguous Road Signs   126-131.
Anger   28.
Answers to Quiz   145-160.
Appropriateness (speed)   23.
Assuming   17. 18. 32. 38.
    48. 50. 141.
    162. 168.
Attitudes   1. 12. 15. 16.
    20. 26. 29. 30.
    32. 37. 48. 50.
    54. 59. 78. 99.
    107.
Authorities (Section 9)   161-169.
Authorities (general)   9. 81.
    161-169.
Authorities in Need
    of Education
    (Section 9)   161-169.
Authors (contact)   169.
Auxiliaries   45.
Awareness (driver)   10. 15. 16. 26.
    41. 66. 87. 91-
    94. 107-108.
    116-117. 120-121.
    146-160. 167-169.

B

Baby on Board (stickers)   14.
Basics (motorway)   66.
Be Ahead of the Game
    (Section 5)   29. 109-118.
Belief   116.
Belisha Beacons   124.
Bends   37. 61- 64.
    151-152.
Black Metal Posts   21.
Blame   18-19.
Blown Off Course
    (motorway)   73.
Blue Background
    Circular Signs   126.
Bonus (it's only a)   10. 27. 70. 87.
    117. 121. 169.
Breakdown   114.
Braking   39. 48. 53-54.
    66. 99.
Bridges   94-95.
Build-Outs (footpath)   21.
Bus   37. 149-150. 163.
Bus Stops   21. 134.
    149-150.

C

Calm & in control   29. 31.
Cameras (speed)   9. 23. 102. 162.
Car Parks   44. 64. 97.
Carriageway Markings   21. 95-96.
'Cat's Eyes'   95-96.
'Cattle' Warning Sign   131.
Celebrities
    (security advice)   110-117.
Centre Lane Owners Club
    (CLOCS)   91-94.
Centrifugal Force   64. 151-152.
Chances   56.
Changing Lanes
    (motorway)   68. 74. 93.
Check Your Distance   80.
Chevrons   81.
Chicanes   133.
'Children' Warning Sign   132.
Circular Road Signs   126-139.
Circumstances Reasonably
    Expected to Develop   35.
Clearways   142.
CLOCS   91-94.
Closing Gaps (motorway)   71-72.
Clutch Pedal   39. 45.
Command position
    on the Road   71-72. 117.
Composure   116.

Computers	102.
Concentration	15. 49.
Confidence	13.
Congestion	16. 163-165.
Cornering (see Bends)	
Council Folly	22. 133-137.
Country Lanes	16. 27. 34. 37.
Courtesy	45-46. 61.
Crashes	17. 20. 83. 162.
Cycle Lanes	21-22. 135-137.
	156.
Cycleway Warning Sign	137.
Cyclists	37. 45-46. 135
	137. 156-157.
Cyclists (motor)	105.

D

Dangerous Roads	19. 168.
Junctions	19.
Bends	19.
Dangles & Distractions	14.
Debris	83-84. 105. 151.
Decisions	10. 107-108. 162.
Department of Transport	14.
Design & Print	2.
Developing an Attitude	
(Section 3)	25-64.
Did You Know?	139-144.
Discipline	116.
Distance (keep your)	80.
Distractions & Dangles	14.
Do's and Don't	113.
Don't Rush	
(gear changing)	40.
Doors & Windows	44. 46.
	154-155.
Double White Lines	142.
Doubt	38.
Driver (The)	10. 13-14
	20-21. 165.
Driver Awareness Ltd.	169.
Driver Awareness	
Summary	
(see Section 6)	119-122.

Drivers: Unskilled	
Arrogant	
Indifferent	
Bad Mannered	
Criminal	27.
Driving Plans	29. 33. 36. 38.
	59. 61. 69. 71.
Dual Carriageways	49.

E

Early Moves	77.
'Easy View' Railings	144.
Education	9-10. 12. 15-16.
	20-21. 23. 27.
	65-66. 77. 81.
	85. 102. 107.
	124. 162. 168.
Eight Blunders	
of the World	13.
'Elderly People'	
Warning Sign	132.
Emerging from	
a Junction	46.
Emission Detectors	103-104.
Entertainment	66. 108.
Everyday Scenarios	37.
Exclamations of Surprise	
(anger)	28. 35. 49. 120.
	167.
Exits – motorway	68. 99.
Experience	12-13.
Expertise	15.
Eyesight	14. 32. 49. 81.
	167.

F

Failing To Plan	33.
Fast Lane Survival	78.
Fatigue (driver)	165.
Fault (whose)	49.
Finding Third	39.
Following	31. 33-34.
	53-57. 66-67.
	71. 80-82.

Folly (council)   22. 133-137.
Footballers (professional)   29. 116-117.
Footpath build-outs   21.
Foreword   9.
'Four-Way' Junctions.   126.
Fume Emission Detectors   103-104.
Future (The)   163-169.

G

General Awareness
   Advice   42.
Gears and Gear Lever   13. 39-40. 44.
'Give Way' Sign (or is it?) 128-129.
Glasses & Contact Lenses 32.
Going Round the Bend   61.

H

Habits   16. 20. 26. 33.
                       120. 168.
Hard Shoulder   85-89.
Hazard Lights   88.
Hazard Perception   167.
Hazards   9. 16. 22. 71. 83.
Hazardous Loads   78-79.
Headlights   106.
High Speed Challenge   100-102.
Horn   106.
How Aware Are You?   41.
Human Nature   18. 24. 44. 72.

I

Idiots on High   94-95.
Impatience   13.
Index for Sections   3.
Indicators
   (see Signals)   37. 45. 141. 159.
Instruction (Driving)   20.
Insurance (vehicle/driver) 16. 167.
Introduction (Section 1) 7-10.

J

Joining the Motorway   67.
Judgment   12.
Junctions
   (see also Roundabouts) 46-47. 59. 68.
                       99. 159.

K

Keep Your Distance   80. 168.

L

'L' Plates   14.
Lack of Consideration   13.
Lampposts   143.
Lane Discipline   91-94.
Lane Use (Restrictions) 78.
Leaders   117. 121. 168.
Learner Drivers   103.
Leaving Your Vehicle   13. 22. 40. 89.
                       97.
Left Hand Drive Vehicles 74-75.
Lights - see Headlights
Loading (Unloading)   140.
Locating Yourself   90-91.
'Long Loads' Sign
   (or is it?)   127.
Lurker (The)   34-35. 59.

M

Making Your Moves   56.
Marginal Strip
   (see Vibra Strip)
Marker Posts   90.
Metal Posts   21.
Matrix Signs   101.
'Midas'   166.
Mini-Roundabouts   126.
Mirrors   4. 59.
Missiles – motorway   66. 70-71. 78.
MOLS   91-94.
Monotony   108. 168.
Motor Cyclists   105. 159.
Motorway Driving
   (Section 4)   65-108.
Motorway Education 107-108.
Motorway Tuition   65.
Motorways (Boring)   108. 168.
Moving Off   45.
'My Offside Lane Society'
   (MOLS)   91-94.

N

Nearside Lanes
  (motorway)   68.
Negatives into positives
  (see Bonus)
Night Time Driving   16.
No Loading/Unloading   140.
'No Right Turn'
'No Left Turn'
'No U Turn' Signs
  (or are they?)   129.
Non-Trust   28. 41. 45. 49.
  66. 70. 95. 120 -
  121. 148. 169.

Number Plates   32.

O

Observations   12. 29-30. 35.
  42. 46. 53-54.
  59. 66. 74.
  76-77. 144.
Obstruction   165.
Offside Lane
  (see Outside Lane)
Opportunities   56.
Outside Lane   86. 91-94. 104.
Over-confidence   13.
Overtaking   16. 27. 35. 54.
  56-61. 75. 77.
  92-94. 135. 165.

Overtaking Simplified   59.

P

Paint   21-22. 47.
  142-143. 156.
Palm Pilot (The)   39.
Parked Vehicles   37. 42-43. 87.
  153-155.
Parking   22. 43-44. 64.
Parking Gear   40.
Parking Sign   127. 130.
Pavement build-outs   21.
Pedal Cyclist
  (see Cyclists)
Pedestrian Crossings   124. 128.
Perimeter Roads   99. 127-128.
Posts (see Marker Posts)

Presuming   168.
Pride   13.
Police   4. 24. 27. 84.
  89-90. 102. 107.
  112. 124-125. 162.
Pollution   16. 163-165.
Positioning   51-53. 58-61. 74.
  151-152.

Posts (see Marker Posts)
Public Eye (people in)   110-112.
Publisher   2.
Punctures   84-85. 89.

Q

Queues   55. 94. 106.
  121. 164.

Quiz & Answers
  (Section.8)   145-160.
Quiz for the Reader   103-106.

R

Railings   144.
Rain   37. 158.
Reaction Time
  (see Thinking Distance)
Reading Number Plates   32.
Red Circle Signs   127-129. 139.
Red Strips   21.
Reflectors
  (see 'Cat's Eyes')
Responsibility
for Yourself   55. 101. 121.
  169.
Reversing   64.
Right Hand Lane
  (see Outside Lane)
Risk (people at special)   110-112.
Road Conditions   48. 158.
Road Markings   21-22.
Road Narrowing   69. 133. 135.
Road Works – motorway   69.
Roads (Dangerous)   19. 168.
'Round' Traffic Signs   127-129.
Roundabouts   50-51. 158.
Rumble Strip
  (see Vibra Strip)

THE **THINKER'S** GUIDE

S

Safety Cameras
    (an inappropriate name for speed cameras)
Satellite Systems   166.
Seat Belts   40.
Security &
    VIP Protection
    (Section 5)   109-118.
Security (general)   97. 110-112. 169.
Self-Assurance   116.
Service Areas   97-98.
Setting Down Passengers   140.
'Sheep' Warning Sign   131.
Signal (Courtesy)   46.
Signals
    (see also Indicators)   45.
Signs (roundabouts)   51.
Signs (general)   80-81. 91. 100-
    101. 126-139.
Simplicity   29. 33.
Slip Roads – motorway   67. 69. 99.
Slippery Road Surfaces   48. 50. 98. 158.
Slipstreaming   48. 166.
'Slow' Road Sign
    (or is it?)   127.
Slow, Timid,
Negative Drivers   14. 26. 72. 77-
    78. 86. 117. 159.
    168.
Skid Causes   48.
Smooooothness   29.
Space   29. 41. 44. 54-
    56. 59. 64. 66-
    68. 70. 74. 117.
    121. 133. 135.
    169.
Speed   14. 22-24. 48.
    61. 100-102.
Speed Cameras   9. 23-24. 102.
    162.
Speed Kills   9. 22-23. 79.
    102. 168.
Speed Limiters   165.
Speed Limits   23-24. 100-102.

Speedometers   24. 48.
Sporting Activity
    (professional)   116-117.
Sporting Comparison   29.
Starting Blocks   26.
Stationary Traffic   106.
Steering   40. 76. 85.
Stickers (and window
    obstructions)   14.
Steve O'Donnell
    About the Authors   5.
Straight Line Steer   76.
Summary (Sec.6)   119-122.
Steering   31. 48.
Stopping a vehicle safely   54. 62. 81.
Straight Lines (steering)   58-59.
Swerving   31.
Synopsis (Section 2)   11-24.

T

'T on T'
    (Tyres on Tarmac)   55.
Telephones
    Mobile   14. 49. 89.
Telephones
    On Motorways   89-90.
Temporary Stops   45.
The Future   163-169.
The Driver   20.
Theft (of and
    from vehicle)   110-112.
Thinking Distance   48. 80.
Three 'V's   52.
Three Wheel Vehicles   103.
Time for a Change   39.
Timid Drivers
    (motorway)   72. 99.
Timidity   26. 117. 159.
Tractors   131. 157.
Traffic Calming   21. 133-136.
168.
Traffic Lights   37. 47-48. 139.
    146-147. 164.

Trust	28. 41. 45. 49. 66. 70. 120-121. 148.
Tuition (Motorway)	65.
Two Second Rule	53-54. 66. 83.
'Two Way Traffic' Sign (or is it?)	128.
Twitching (the steering wheel)	31.
Tyre Troubles	84-85. 99. 158.
Tyres	61.

U

Unaware Driver	28.

V

'V's (three)	52.
Vascar	102.
Vehicle Abuse	13.
Vehicle Emission Detectors	103-104.
Vehicle Technology	19.
Vehicle Theft	110-112.
Vibra Strip	89. 105.
VIP Protection & Security (Section 5)	109-118.
VIP Protection Attitudes	27-28. 110-112. 148. 169.
Visual Aids	32.

W

Warning Signs	129. 131-132. 157.
Website	169.
Weather (Accidents)	168.
Weather Conditions	18. 27. 36. 73. 106.
Weight Distribution (vehicle)	61. 73. 151-152.
What do you Think? (Section 7)	123-144.
What if?	35-36. 43. 46. 148-149. 169.
What People Say	6.
What to Look for	30.
White Lines	142-143.
White Squares	102.
Windows & Doors	42-46.
Windy Conditions (motorway)	73.

Y

Yellow Boxes	47-48. 146.
Yellow Lines	140.

Z

Zones of Invisibility	35-37. 148.